P9-CJE-688

YO-YO MA

ASIAN AMERICANS
OF ACHIEVEMENT

Margaret Cho

Daniel Inouye

Michelle Kwan

Bruce Lee

Maya Lin

Yo-Yo Ma

Isamu Noguchi

Amy Tan

Vera Wang

Kristi Yamaguchi

ASIAN AMERICANS OF ACHIEVEMENT

YO-YO MA

RICHARD WORTH

CHELSEA HOUSE
P U B L I S H E R S

An imprint of Infobase Publishing

921
MA

Yo-Yo Ma

Chelsea House
An imprint of Infobase Publishing
132 West 31st Street
New York, NY 10001

Library of Congress Cataloging-in-Publication Data
Worth, Richard.
 Yo-yo Ma / Richard Worth.
    p. cm. — (Asian Americans of achievement)
 Includes bibliographical references and index.
 ISBN 978-0-7910-9270-5 (hardcover)
 1. Ma, Yo-Yo, 1955—Juvenile literature. 2. Violoncellists—Biography—Juvenile literature. I. Title. II. Series.
 ML3930.M11W67 2006
 787.4092—dc22
 [B]   2006026335

Chelsea House books are available at special discounts when purchased in bulk quantities for businesses, associations, institutions, or sales promotions. Please call our Special Sales Department in New York at (212) 967-8800 or (800) 322-8755.

You can find Chelsea House on the World Wide Web at
http://www.chelseahouse.com

Series design by Erika K. Arroyo
Cover design by Ben Peterson

Printed in the United States of America

Bang EJB 10 9 8 7 6 5 4 3 2 1

This book is printed on acid-free paper.

All links and Web addresses were checked and verified to be correct at the time of publication. Because of the dynamic nature of the Web, some addresses and links may have changed since publication and may no longer be valid.

CONTENTS

Yo-Yo Ma
in Concert

On the stage of London's Barbican Centre in December 2005, a lone performer sat in front of a huge, sold-out audience. Between his knees was a polished cello. In one hand he held the neck of the cello, with its four strings. The other hand grasped a long bow. As the audience waited in hushed silence, the performer slowly drew his bow across the strings of the cello.

The music that evening was the Six Suites for Unaccompanied Cello, written almost three centuries earlier by German composer Johann Sebastian Bach. The six suites are considered among the most beautiful works ever composed for the solo cello, and possibly the most difficult. Every great cellist is expected to master them. No cellist has played them any better than the performer who sat on the London stage that December—Yo-Yo Ma.

As Ma began to play Suite no. 1, the music floated through the air, filling the magnificent Barbican Centre. Yo-Yo Ma first learned to play the Bach suites when he was a child. According to author David Blum, Ma was taught the suites by his father,

The main foyer of the Barbican Centre in London is shown here. Yo-Yo Ma performed Bach's cello suites at the Barbican in 2005. Bach's music has a special significance for Ma.

Hiao-Tsiun Ma, a violinist and music teacher. "Each day, Yo-Yo was expected to memorize two measures [groups of notes] of Bach; the following day, two more measures. He learned to recognize patterns—their similarities and their differences—and soon developed a feeling for musical structure. By the time he was five, he had learned three Bach suites."

Yo-Yo's father learned the suites while he was living in Paris during World War II (1939–1945). The Germans conquered France in 1940 and occupied Paris, the French capital. Ma's father lived alone during the occupation. During the war, according to Ma, his father

> . . . would memorize violin pieces by Bach and play them in the dark. He eventually advised me to follow his example and play through a Bach suite from memory every night before going to bed. . . . I know my greatest joy as a musician when I am playing a concert dedicated exclusively to Bach. Then for a whole evening I'm living in one man's mind—and a great man's mind.

Yo-Yo Ma was born in Paris in 1955. Hiao-Tsiun Ma taught his son to play the cello when he was only four years old, and the boy memorized three of the Bach cello suites a year later. Ma was considered a child prodigy, that is, a musical genius.

As the concert at the Barbican continued, Ma transitioned from the First Suite to Suite no. 2. Yo-Yo Ma had recorded the complete suites in 1983. For his virtuoso performance, he won a Grammy Award for the best classical music instrumental solo.

Each of the Bach suites written for solo cello has six parts, or movements. The first movement is a prelude, or introduction. In the First Suite the prelude opens "like light becoming stronger," according to Ma. "I feel that I'm out in nature." The prelude in each of the suites is followed by four dances—an allemande, a courante, a sarabande, and a minuet. These dances were popular in Europe during the eighteenth century. The

Yo-Yo Ma is considered by many to be the one of the finest cellists in the world. His father recognized his son's gift and started the boy on the violin at an early age.

final part is a gigue, derived from the word *jig,* a dance popular in England during the same period.

Ma won a Grammy Award for his recording of Bach's suites when he was only in his twenties, an extremely young age for a classical performer. As author John Attanas pointed out, however, Ma had a head start on many other performers.

> Because of the difficulty of the notes and because of the emotional and intellectual depth of the suites, most music teachers will not assign them to a student until the student has both the technique to master the fingering, and the life experience to have some insight into what Bach is writing about.

Yo-Yo Ma's father knew that his son was gifted and taught him the suites much earlier than other cellists had learned them.

After completing the Second Suite, Ma began Suite no. 3. The Third Suite, like the others, has very difficult chords. These require precise fingering by the cellist, and no one is more experienced at playing these chords than Ma. Cellists like Yo-Yo Ma have helped make the Third Suite "the most popular of all," according to David Blum.

While the Third Suite is "noble and exuberant," according to Ma, he describes the Fourth Suite as one that reaches new heights for the solo cello. "When I am playing this, I feel that the cello becomes an orchestra or an organ." The Fifth Suite, for Ma, is "the most profound of all the suites." It expresses the sadness felt by the composer. Ma's solo performance concludes with Suite no. 6. According to Ma, the last suite "is exalted, and celebrates the glory of life."

As Yo-Yo Ma completed the final suite, the London audience exploded into a standing ovation. Ma rose from his chair on stage and bowed to the appreciative crowd. It was another triumph for the man considered one of the greatest cellists ever to play on the world stage.

2

Family Background and Early Life

Yo-Yo Ma's family has deep roots in China. Hiao-Tsiun Ma, Yo-Yo Ma's father, was born in 1911 outside Shanghai, a city in eastern China. Shanghai is a large seaport, located on the Yangtze River and the East China Sea. Hiao-Tsiun Ma's father was a prosperous landowner. He was determined that his son receive an education, which held the key to a successful career in China. The educational system had recently been opened up to accommodate more students. Several million were studying in new schools that had been started across the country.

Hiao-Tsiun Ma took his place among the other students, when he possessed unusual musical ability and had already learned to play the violin. Encouraged by his father and his instructors in school, Hiao-Tsiun Ma continued his education and eventually became a music teacher at Nanking University during the 1930s. Nanking is located about 150 miles (240 kilometers) from Shanghai, along the Yangtze River.

THE POLITICAL SITUATION IN CHINA

Throughout the early decades of Hiao-Tsiun Ma's life, China was torn apart by civil war. In 1911, the year of his birth, a revolt occurred at Wuchang in northern China against the centuries-old Chinese monarchy. By the beginning of the following year, China had become a republic, and the emperor was replaced by a president. Political leaders named Dr. Sun Yat-sen as the first president of the Republic of China. For years, Dr. Sun had been a leader in the revolutionary movement to overthrow the monarchy.

Dr. Sun believed strongly in freedom and equality for all Chinese people. He wanted the government of the emperor—run by one person—to be replaced by an elected National Assembly. He did not, however, have the support of all of the political groups inside China. Many powerful warlords refused to take orders from Dr. Sun's government, and civil war erupted across the country over the next decade. In 1921, Dr. Sun established a new government in Canton, located in southern China. He also made an alliance with the Chinese Communists, a newly formed political group. With their help, he hoped to unite southern and northern China under a single government.

Dr. Sun died in 1925 before he could realize his dream. He was succeeded by one of his associates, General Chiang Kai-shek. A year later, Chiang led his soldiers north and took control of the large Chinese cities of Shanghai and Nanking. At first, Chiang cooperated with the Communists, but in 1927, he began a military effort to oust them from China. From his capital in Nanking, Chiang and the Communists engaged in a bloody civil war for control of the vast Chinese nation.

While this war was under way, the Japanese launched an attack on China in 1931. The Japanese invasion began in Manchuria, part of northern China. While civil war raged in the south, Japan conquered Manchuria and established its own government there. Manchuria had rich deposits of coal and oil that Japan needed to run its industries as well as the armed ships and fighter planes that made up its powerful war machine. From Manchuria, Japanese armies headed south toward Nanking.

HIAO-TSIUN AND YA-WEN LO

Nanking, located on the Yangtze River, is an ancient city surrounded by hills. In the 1930s, the city's workers were famous for producing fine handicrafts, such as satins and velvets. Nanking was also home to a large university, where Hiao-Tsiun Ma held his music classes. As the Japanese advanced toward the city, many people began to flee to other parts of China. Afraid that the war would spread farther south, Hiao-Tsiun Ma decided to leave China for the West. He traveled to Paris, where many Chinese students had gone to study.

The Japanese conquered Nanking in 1937. They pillaged the city, killing as many as 300,000 people. Meanwhile, the university moved southward to Chungking. The climate is much milder in Chungking, an old city with winding narrow streets and bamboo houses. The University of Nanking reopened as Central University. When Hiao-Tsiun Ma heard of the reopening, he came back to China from his brief stay in Paris to resume his duties as a music teacher.

One of his students was a young woman named Ya-Wen Lo. She was born in Hong Kong in 1923, the daughter of a well-to-do merchant who sold rice and fish. Hong Kong, boasting one of the world's finest harbors, was a British colony located on the South China Sea. Like Hiao-Tsiun Ma's family, Ya-Wen Lo's parents were strong believers in education for their daughter. She took the entrance examinations for Central University in Chungking and was admitted as a freshman student in the late 1930s.

Ya-Wen Lo was a talented music student. Her focus was opera, and her goal, she said, "was to become a lyric soprano."

Nanking Road, the principal thoroughfare of Shanghai, is shown after a state of siege was declared in 1937.

According to Ya-Wen Lo, she was almost instantly attracted to her tall, dark-haired teacher, Hiao-Tsiun Ma. Among her class-mates at the university was Ma's sister, Tsiun-Cheng. The two women became friendly, and Ya-Wen Lo told Professor Ma's sister that she was interested in finding out more about him. After describing Professor Ma's life, his sister added, "No, he doesn't have a fiancée. Do you really like him that much?" Ya-Wen Lo confessed that she did.

At this time, Japanese armies were conquering more of the Chinese mainland. The government of Chiang Kai-shek moved to Chungking, which was bombed by Japanese planes. The war proved too great a distraction for many students in Professor Ma's classes. Although he tried to persuade his students to work harder, they did not listen. Finally, Hiao-Tsiun Ma gave up and resigned from the university, returning to Paris. Ya-Wen Lo remained in Chunking, where she continued her education. The city turned out to be safer than her homeland, Hong Kong. This city fell to the Japanese in December 1941, soon after their attack on the American naval base at Pearl Harbor, Hawaii. So many people who lived in Hong Kong headed to southern China to escape the Japanese that the population of Hong Kong was reduced by more than half.

PARIS

Ya-Wen Lo remained in Chunking until 1945. Meanwhile, World War II raged across Europe and the Pacific. The United States, Great Britain, and their allies eventually defeated Germany and Japan. After the Japanese surrendered in 1945, Ya-Wen Lo returned to Hong Kong to spend time with her family. She did not intend to remain in Hong Kong indefinitely, however. Her plan was to leave China and travel to Paris with Tsiun-Cheng Ma, who was hoping to join her brother. Ya-Wen Lo hoped to see him, too.

In the late 1940s, both women left Hong Kong for France. Soon after arriving in Paris, Tsiun-Cheng Ma introduced Ya-Wen Lo to Hiao-Tsiun Ma. Ya-Wen Lo noticed that "he seemed unduly stern. . .a trait which gave her strong misgivings. . . . She soon dismissed these thoughts preferring to dwell upon his finer qualities, which overshadowed this trait." Indeed, "she did not fail to miss the twinkle in his eyes as he spoke to her. . . . Realizing how much their backgrounds were alike and how music would fill their souls with happiness," she grew to love him. The couple was eventually married on July 17, 1949.

Their early years of marriage in Paris were a struggle. Ya-Wen took the French name Marina and became a student at Ecole Française, where she continued to study voice. Ma was studying for his Ph.D. degree at the Paris Conservatory of Music.

He and his wife were permitted to live in an apartment owned by the conservatory, which also gave him a small amount of money for instructing students. It was barely enough to survive. Their struggle became even more difficult in 1951, when their first child, a daughter, was born. The Mas' daughter was named Yeou-Cheng, which means "May you have lots of friends." She was also given a French name, Marie-Thérèse.

When she was still a child, it became clear that Yeou-Cheng Ma had inherited a talent for music from her parents. Her father began to teach young Yeou-Cheng the violin when she was only two-and-a-half years old. "I could play violin before I could jump rope," she recalled. "I entered my first competition when I was three and a half, the beginners level. I went with my violin and my bottle, and though I was competing with kids of fourteen and nineteen, I won, to everybody's stupefaction." Yeou-Cheng also learned to play the piano under her father's guidance.

Yeou-Chen's violin teacher praised her work when she was a student of four years old. She told the child's mother, "Your daughter is a brilliant musician. I'm sure you're aware of that. There's no doubt in my mind that she inherits this talent from you and your husband. . . . It's in her genes." Then she added, "Mrs. Ma, what I'm trying to tell you is that I think it is a great pity that you don't plan on having another child." Ya-Wen was astounded at what the teacher was saying. "And where would I put another child. . . ."

The Ma family lived in a small apartment with barely enough room for the couple and their daughter. Ya-Wen Ma soon discovered, however, that her husband also wanted another child. As she put it, "He yearned to have a son who would continue the family name." Sons were highly prized in traditional Chinese society to carry on family traditions and lead the family into the next generation. On October 7, 1955, Ya-Wen Ma gave birth to a seven-and-one-half-pound son, named Yo-Yo and also named Earnest. Yo-Yo means "friendly, friendly," in Chinese, and Ma means "horse." In China, he would have been known as Ma Yo-Yo—his last name would have been placed ahead of his first name.

A CHILD PRODIGY

From his early childhood, Yo-Yo heard music. His sister and father played the violin. His mother was an opera singer. Classical music albums were constantly playing at home. At age three, Yo-Yo began to study the violin. As his sister Yeou-Cheng recalled, "He really hated it. He busted up a couple of them. Then we tried piano, and he wrecked a couple of keys. . . . But then he saw a. . .jazz band, and he totally fell in love with the double bass and said, 'I want that one.'"

JOHANN SEBASTIAN BACH (1865–1750)

Johann Sebastian Bach was one of the greatest classical composers in Western music. Bach came from a family of musicians. His father played in a small orchestra at the palace of the local duke. Bach's brother, Johann Christoph Bach, was a well-known organist who played in the German town of Ohrdruf. Bach was born in Eisenach, Germany, where he began to learn music at an early age from his father and his brother. Bach attended school in Lüneburg, Germany, where he sang in the choir. He also studied music and listened to local organists at churches in the area.

By the early eighteenth century, Bach had become a skilled organist as well as a violinist and played in the orchestra of a German noble, the Prince of Weimar. By age 18, Bach had been appointed as the organist at a church in Arnstadt, where he continued to play until 1707, afterward becoming organist at Blasius Church in Mühlhausen. In Mühlhausen, located in central Germany, he married Maria Barbara Bach, his cousin. Bach also began to compose cantatas, which are pieces for musicians and singers. One of Bach's major responsibilities in Mühlhausen was to

According to his mother, Yo-Yo was a stubborn child who knew what he wanted and had the persistence to keep asking for it. The double bass is a huge instrument, much too big for a child of four years old, however. Instead, Dr. Ma decided to give Yo-Yo an opportunity to play the cello. He bought a small cello, so little that Yo-Yo could handle it.

The violincello, or cello, was developed in Europe during the seventeenth century. It was especially popular with Italian musicians, among the leading performers in western Europe. Since its invention, the cello became part of classical music orchestras and smaller musical groups, such as quartets and quintets. Composers also created pieces of classical music that featured solos by cellists. Like the violin, the cello has four strings, but it is a

perform music for the church services. In addition to the cantatas, Bach also wrote several organ compositions.

A year after coming to Mühlhausen, Bach left to accept a better position as the organist at the court of the Prince of Weimar in central Germany. By 1714, he had been appointed concertmaster, in charge of the prince's orchestra, during which time he composed additional cantatas. In 1717, Bach accepted a new position once again, becoming the musical director in Köthen. His wife, Maria, died in Köthen in 1720, and a year later Bach married Anna Magdalena Wulken. Meanwhile, Bach composed his Six Cello Suites. He also completed a series of six concertos for a local prince, the Elector of Brandenburg. These so-called Brandenburg Concertos are among the most widely played pieces of music by modern orchestras.

Bach remained in Köthen until 1723, when he moved to Leipzig, becoming music director of the Church of St. Thomas. Bach remained in Leipzig until the end of his career and composed some of his most famous music there. His works included religious pieces, the Italian Concerto, compositions for piano, as well as chorales, which are pieces for church choirs.

much larger instrument. A cellist cannot hold the cello and play it. Instead, the performer puts the cello between his or her legs. At the end of the instrument is a long piece of metal called an endpin, which rests on the floor.

Like the violin, the cello is constructed of wood. The strings stretch over the main body of the cello, down the neck of the instrument to a pegbox. This contains four pegs, each controlling one of the strings. With the pegbox, a cellist can tighten or loosen each of the strings to tune it. At the top of the cello is a piece of wood called the scroll, so named because of its shape. To produce music, a cellist uses one hand to draw the bow across the strings near the bridge, which raises the strings at the center of the cello. Meanwhile, the cellist moves the fingers of the other hand along the strings on the neck of the cello. Two f-shaped holes have been carved—one to the right and one to the left of the bridge. Air circulates from outside and inside the instrument through the holes, enabling the sound of the cello to fill a music hall.

When Dr. Ma began to teach Yo-Yo to play the Bach cello suites, he taught the composition in small, bite-sized pieces. Dr. Ma realized that this was the best way for children to learn. If they tried to master too much of a piece of music, they became bored and discouraged. Yo-Yo memorized a few notes on one day and then added a few more notes the next day. Eventually, he had memorized an entire cello suite and could play it without looking at the music.

Yo-Yo's success was also due in large part to his inborn musical talent. Harold Schonberg, the former music critic for the *New York Times,* wrote that

> certain children . . . are born with an order of ear, memory, reflex, synthesis, intelligence, and instinct that far separates them from normal children. These children are the ones who are going to become the great perform-

ers. (It is hard to think of an outstanding pianist or violinist who started after six years of age. . . .)

Yo-Yo was one of these children. By the age of five, he was
already playing several compositions by Bach. According to
Marina Ma, her husband "set forth certain well-defined guidelines for his son's intellectual development. He stressed organi-
zation, concentration, memorization, constant practice, and, at
the head of them all, discipline. Mistakes were acceptable during practice but not at the final performances." Dr. Ma realized,
though, that, because he was not a cellist, he could take his son's
musical education only so far. After Dr. Ma had instilled his
own approach to music, he then found his son a cello teacher
who could help him take his skills as a cellist to the next level.

In Paris, Yo-Yo was introduced to his new teacher, Made-
moiselle Michelle Lepinte. During their first lesson, he played a
piece by Bach. Lepinte was amazed that Yo-Yo was able to master such a difficult composition. Soon after she began to work
with him, though, Lepinte realized what an unusual student Yo-
Yo was. "He was clearly not an average talent to be nurtured at
an average pace," according to Ma's biographer John Attanas.
"Rather, he was a prodigy, and should be allowed to develop at
his own pace, even if that was a swift one."

Just before his sixth birthday, Yo-Yo took part in a recital
that included pieces to be played by Michelle Lepinte's students.
Held at the University of Paris Institute of Art and Archeology,
the recital was given in front of an audience filled with parents
and relatives of the music students. Yo-Yo was expected to play
two short pieces and then leave the stage. After he had finished
a small selection from a Bach cello suite, however, Yo-Yo did
not want to stop. He enjoyed the audience's applause. He played
several more selections, stopping after each one as the audience
applauded. Finally, he completed his performance to a huge
ovation. Even as a child, Yo-Yo loved to perform in front of
large audiences.

3

The Ma Family Comes to America

Marina Ma and her husband did not always agree on the best way to guide their son's growth as a musician. Both of them recognized that he was unusually gifted, but Marina was willing to give Yo-Yo the freedom to develop on his own. She was not sure that he should strive for a career as a musician. As she told her husband, "We both have studied music and pray tell me, where has it got us? We can't even make ends meet." Dr. Ma disagreed with her. "I'm going to make a musician out of him," he said.

Dr. Ma believed that Yo-Yo's life should be carefully structured around music. His focus must be practice, memorization, and the development of his technique as a gifted cellist. This was the only way for him to realize his full potential as a musician. Eventually, Marina came around to her husband's way of thinking as she watched her son play, saw his fingers handle the bow as it glided across the strings of his cello, and listened as he produced beautiful music while he was still a child.

RENDEZVOUS WITH DESTINY

What neither of Yo-Yo's parents could guess was that his future would not be nurtured in Paris. Although it was a center of culture with many opportunities for musicians, Paris would not be the place where Yo-Yo's future lay. Instead, it would be across the Atlantic Ocean in the United States—more specifically, in New York City.

The series of events that led the Mas to the United States began with a package that Marina Ma received from her sister, who lived in California. As Marina explained in her biography, the package contained some fortune cookies. She broke open one of the cookies and inside was a message that read, "You will soon embark on a long voyage."

Shortly afterward, Dr. Ma received a letter from his brother, Hiao-Jone Ma, who lived in Rochester, New York. Hiao-Jone Ma had hoped that the United States would be a land of opportunity for him when he moved there many years earlier, but he had been disappointed. As a result, he was thinking of returning to China. Dr. Ma believed that his brother's decision was a terrible mistake. The government of Chiang Kai-shek had been driven out of China by the Communists in 1949. Led by Mao Zedong, the Communists had imposed a brutal dictatorship on China. Anyone who disagreed with the government was imprisoned or executed.

Dr. Ma and his brother were part of a close-knit family, an important element in Chinese traditions. Dr. Ma tried to write to his brother and make a long-distance telephone call to Rochester to plead with him not to return to China. Dr. Ma feared for his brother's life. When Hiao-Jone Ma still seemed unconvinced, Dr. Ma decided to fly to New York with his entire family. Scraping together what little money he had, Dr. Ma bought airplane tickets and brought his family to New York City. Then they traveled northward to Rochester, located on Lake Erie.

There they joined Dr. Ma's brother. It was a new experience for Dr. Ma and his family, who spoke very little English.

Eventually, Dr. Ma succeeded in talking Hiao-Jone Ma out of returning to China. Although his attention had been focused on his brother, Dr. Ma had not forgotten about his son, Yo-Yo. In Rochester, Dr. Ma contacted nearby Nazareth College and arranged for Yo-Yo and his sister to play a concert. It included several pieces for cello and piano as well as a Bach cello suite. The audience applauded loudly at the end of the concert. After a short stay in Rochester, Marina Ma wanted to visit her sister in Berkeley, California. After the Mas arrived there, Marina asked her sister, "Do you remember those cookies you sent me? Well, my 'fortune' did come true."

The Mas had planned only a short visit to America, but Dr. Ma was drawn to New York City, one of the world's great centers of classical music. At Carnegie Hall, built by the great American industrialist Andrew Carnegie in 1892, some of the twentieth century's finest musicians had played to a packed house. Dr. Ma hoped that his son Yo-Yo might some day join them.

A JOB AT TRENT SCHOOL

In New York City, Dr. Ma found a small apartment for his family. To remain in the United States, though, seemed out of the question, at first. The family was short of money, and Dr. Ma had no job. Nevertheless, news of the concert that Yo-Yo and his sister played in Rochester had traveled to New York City. As a result, Dr. Ma was successful in arranging for Yo-Yo and his sister to play a small concert there. Attending the concert was Ms. Isalina Davidson, the director of the Trent School in New York. Davdson enjoyed the concert, and she was especially impressed with the high quality of the performance by Yo-Yo and his sister. She also hoped that the students at her private school might be taught to perform at similar events.

After hearing Yo-Yo and his sister play, Isalina Davidson approached Dr. Ma. She asked him if he would like a job as the

Spanish cellist, conductor, and composer Pablo Casals, a musician who helped popularize classical cello music is pictured here. Casals was responsible for arranging Yo-Yo Ma's performance for President John F. Kennedy.

music teacher and orchestra director at the Trent School. Dr. Ma accepted the offer and began to prepare for his family to live permanently in the United States. Before they could make the transition, the Mas returned to Paris briefly to gather their possessions and close up their apartment.

While they were in Paris, Yo-Yo and his sister continued to be instructed by Dr. Ma and followed their schedule of intense practice. In addition, Dr. Ma dedicated himself to instilling Chinese culture into his two children. Yo-Yo grew up speaking Chinese and learning to write the Chinese language. His parents never wanted him to lose touch with his ancient heritage. While living in Paris, Dr. Ma also bought a small house outside the city. He hoped that his family might return periodically to France during vacations. Although Dr. Ma had very little money, he received some financial help from his brother in Rochester. The house needed repairs, but a friend offered to get the work done at very low cost.

While they were still in Paris, however, a serious accident befell Yo-Yo. While trying to open a window in the apartment, his hand went through the pane of glass, and he received a severe gash on his wrist. Eventually, Marina slowed the bleeding, and a neighbor took Yo-Yo and his mother to the hospital. Fortunately, the cut was treated in the hospital's emergency department, and no lasting damage was done to Yo-Yo's hand.

NEW YORK CITY

In 1962, Yo-Yo and his family returned to New York. He and his sister were enrolled in the Trent School, and Dr. Ma took up his duties as music teacher. Both children learned English, worked on their studies, and continued to practice. An old joke goes like this: A visitor to New York City asks a passerby how to get to Carnegie Hall. The answer is "Practice! Practice! Practice!" Although Yo-Yo was not yet ready to appear on the stage of the famed concert hall, he was making progress. It was not always easy. Like any boy of eight, Yo-Yo liked to have fun. "Practice! Practice! Practice!" was not his idea of a good time, no matter how much his father told him that it was the only way to improve his playing. His mother recalled that Yo-Yo was an impish little boy, who often tried to distract his older sister from practicing by playing games. Once, he shot spitballs into the room where she was playing; Dr. Ma later caught him and became very angry.

AN UNUSUAL OPPORTUNITY

While Yo-Yo and his family were living in New York, Dr. Ma was introduced to Alexander Schneider, a well-known classical musician who played with the Budapest Quartet. When Schneider heard Yo-Yo play the cello, he was highly impressed with the child's performance. He asked Dr. Ma if Yo-Yo had ever met Pablo Casals, the twentieth century's greatest cellist. Yo-Yo had listened to Casals's recordings and greatly admired the famed cellist. Schneider, who was a friend of Casals's, arranged for Yo-Yo to play for him in New York.

The little boy and his father went to the hotel where Casals was living. After being introduced to the great cellist, Yo-Yo began to play. After Yo-Yo finished the piece, Casals asked him if he would like to continue to play. Yo-Yo continued on, and Casals delighted in the music that was being produced by such a small boy. After the performance had ended, Casals told Dr. Ma about a program of classical music soon to be presented in Washington, D.C. Casals said that he would arrange for Yo-Yo and his sister to play in the program.

Late in November 1962, Yo-Yo and his sister appeared on stage at the Washington National Armory with other performers. Among those seated in the audience were President John F. Kennedy and his wife, Jacqueline. Although Yo-Yo admitted to being a little nervous, he played brilliantly. The *Washington Post* praised his performance. Two years later, he performed Cello Concerto no.1 by French composer Camille Saint-Saëns in New York City.

PABLO CASALS (1876–1973)

Pablo Casals was a famed cellist who helped popularize classical cello music during his long career. Born in Spain, Casals's early life was much like Yo-Yo Ma's. Casals was taught to play the violin at age three by his father—an organist—but soon afterward decided to exchange his violin for a cello. In 1888, Casals attended the Municipal School of Music in Barcelona, Spain, where he studied cello music. Among his best-known cello pieces was Bach's Suites for Solo Cello. Casals began to play them when he was 13 years old. According to author Marshall C. St. John, Casals's father had come to Barcelona, where his son was attending school. He was also playing at a café to earn some extra money.

> At a small, dusty old music store . . . near Barcelona's harbor, Pablo discovered some cello sonatas by Beethoven, and the Bach Suites. He was familiar with Bach, of course. . . . But he had never before seen these Bach suites, now so familiar to all cellists. He had not even known they existed! Now, as he saw them for the first time in his life, he was immediately enthralled and absorbed by them. He read through all the Suites as soon as he arrived home. For the rest of his life he practiced and played the Suites daily. . . .

By the late nineteenth century, Casals was an internationally recognized star. He played for the Spanish royal family in Madrid, Spain, and later for Queen Victoria, the English monarch. During the early part of the twentieth century, Casals traveled to the United States, where, in 1904, he played a concert for President Theodore Roosevelt at the White House. During the 1920s, Casals led his own orchestra in Barcelona. He left Spain in the 1930s, however, after the country fell under the control of dictator Francisco Franco. Casals never returned. He died in Puerto Rico at age 96.

Violinist Isaac Stern (*left*) introduced Yo-Yo Ma to cellist Leonard Rose (*right*). Stern and Rose are seen here playing in a trio with pianist Eugene Istomin in 1961.

ISAAC STERN AND A NEW INSTRUCTOR

Dr. Ma remained at the Trent School, which later merged with another private school and became known as the Ecole Française. In 1964, the Ecole Française staged a fund-raising benefit concert at Carnegie Hall. Featured in the program was Diahann Carroll, a well-known, popular vocalist, and the famed classical violinist Isaac Stern. Stern played a piece by Russian composer Pyotr Tchaikovsky, and another composition by French composer Camille Saint-Saëns. Yo-Yo and his sister were also featured on the program, playing a sonata for cello and piano by composer G.B. Sammartini. According to a review that appeared the next day in the *New York Times,* their performance "had assurance, poise, and a full measure of delicate musicality."

Isaac Stern was very impressed with Yo-Yo's performance. Born in 1920 in Russia, Stern came to the United States with his parents when he was only a year old. He first learned the piano but eventually turned to the violin. Stern attended classes at the San Francisco Conservatory and appeared as a soloist with the San Francisco Symphony in 1935, at the age of 15. Four years later, he appeared on the New York stage. This began an international career that continued for six decades.

The violinist had first heard Yo-Yo play in Paris several years earlier. "I could sense then, as has now been confirmed, that he has one of the most extraordinary talents of his generation," Stern said. Shortly after the performance, Stern approached Dr. Ma to talk about Yo-Yo's future. Up until the concert, Yo-Yo had been studying with cello teacher János Sholz. Stern believed that it was time for the boy to change teachers. He suggested Leonard Rose. Considered a great cellist, Rose played in a trio along with Stern and pianist Eugene Istomin. Yo-Yo's career would now move into its next stage, under the direction of Leonard Rose, with some help from Isaac Stern.

4

Teenage
Years

As a gifted young musician, Yo-Yo Ma experienced an adolescence that was not the same as that of other young people. For example, many teenagers engaged in sports, like soccer, baseball, or basketball. Yo-Yo's parents did not allow him to participate in any athletic activities. He might injure his hands, which could mean an end to his playing.

Marina Ma told a story about a trip to Connecticut that the family took one summer. They had gone to visit Dr. John Rallo and his family. Dr. Rallo had been a colleague of Dr. Ma's at the Ecole Française and later helped Marina write her book on Yo-Yo, titled *My Son, Yo-Yo*. The Rallos had two sons, Chris and John-Peter, who played with Yo-Yo when he came to visit. One day, Chris asked Yo-Yo to go fishing with him. Although Yo-Yo wanted to fish, Dr. Ma would not allow it. While baiting his hook, Yo-Yo might have an accident and injure his fingers. As a compromise, Chris and Yo-Yo were permitted to go for a walk in the park. When they arrived near a river, Chris had an idea. He baited Yo-Yo's hook for him so he could go fishing. This enabled Yo-Yo to do what he wanted without risking his musical career and disappointing his father.

Yo-Yo's mother and father felt responsible for nurturing the talent that their son possessed. This meant that Yo-Yo had to avoid activities that were enjoyed by many other teenagers and, instead, spend countless hours practicing his music, often guided by his father. Yo-Yo was expected to practice in the morning before school and in the evening before going to bed.

Dr. Ma maintained a studio in the apartment building downstairs from where the Ma family lived. He gave music lessons in the studio and trained the Children's Orchestra of New York, which regularly gave performances in the city. Dr. Ma founded the orchestra during the 1960s—the first permanent orchestra made up of children. Yo-Yo and his sister played in the orchestra and inspired other young children with their music.

Dr. Ma expected Yo-Yo's playing to set an example for the other children in the orchestra. He knew that Yo-Yo's gift enabled him to play with the skill of a professional and wanted him to practice each piece until it was perfect. When he was not playing with his father, Yo-Yo was working with cellist Leonard Rose. As Isaac Stern recalled, Rose "told me that, unlike any other student he could remember, Yo-Yo would come to every lesson perfectly prepared. It's not just that he had practiced. He played every piece from memory and had obviously worked constantly on everything he had been assigned. He bloomed under Lenny."

Before taking lessons from Rose, Yo-Yo had become comfortable with his earlier cello teacher, János Scholz. At first, he was in awe of Leonard Rose. "I was a pipsqueak of a kid and overwhelmingly shy," he recalled in David Blum's *Quintet*. "I was afraid to speak to Mr. Rose above a whisper. I'd try to hide behind the cello. He was always calm, soothing, and gentle."

At the time that Yo-Yo was studying with Rose, the Ma family made a trip to San Francisco to visit Marina's sister.

YO-YO MA'S CELLO TEACHERS

After coming to the United States, Yo-Yo Ma had two cello teachers. The first was János Scholz (1903–1993). Scholz was born in Hungary into a family that had produced generation after generation of professional cellists. He graduated from the Royal Hungarian Academy of Music in Budapest, the capital of Hungary. Afterward, Scholz played with the Budapest Symphony Orchestra and the Budapest Opera. In 1933, he arrived in the United States on a tour with a string quartet. To escape the coming of Nazism in Europe, Scholz decided to stay and became a U.S. citizen. Scholz later said that he arrived with only "a suitcase and a cello." He continued to play in the United States throughout the rest of his career, while also building a reputation as a gifted cello teacher.

Leonard Rose (1918–1984) was Yo-Yo Ma's second teacher in the United States. Born in Washington, D.C., Rose inherited his musical gifts from his father, a cellist, who taught his son to play. At age 18, Rose began to play with the NBC Symphony Orchestra, under the leadership of renowned conductor Arturo Toscanini. Later, Rose joined the Cleveland Symphony and in 1943 became the principal cellist with the New York Philharmonic. Eventually, Rose left the orchestra to devote himself to playing as a cello soloist, as well as recording music and teaching. He was considered one of the best American teachers and musicians of the twentieth century. He trained many outstanding cellists, among them Lynn Harrell and Yo-Yo Ma. As Harrell said, "He had a wonderful way to make you play better that was not methodology, but he gave you confidence. He made you feel good about yourself when you were doing it." Yo-Yo Ma added, "One of the marks of a great teacher lies not only in an ability to impart knowledge but also in knowing when to encourage a student to go off on his own." Rose urged Ma to try out new pieces on his own, which enabled him to become an even greater cellist.

Because of Yo-Yo's success in New York, he was asked to play with the San Francisco Symphony Orchestra. A review of Yo-Yo's performance said that, as a young man of only 12, he was already playing as well as his teacher, Leonard Rose. Yo-Yo could have performed with other orchestras as a boy. His father, however, was careful not to push him into a career too early. Dr. Ma did not want his son to become stressed out before he had perfected his skills and become a world-class cellist.

Instead, he returned to New York to continue to practice with Leonard Rose, who was already impressed with his abilities. "He may have one of the greatest techniques of all time," Rose once said. "I'm always floored by it." Rose was preparing Yo-Yo for his first solo recital at Carnegie Hall. Meanwhile, he performed in a concert at the United Nations in New York, early in 1971. He also gave a recital in Boston with the Harvard-Radcliffe Orchestra. His sister, Yeou-Cheng, was attending Radcliffe College there at the time.

Yo-Yo's first recital at Carnegie Hall, the most prestigious concert hall in the United States, took place in 1971, when he was only 15. The hall was packed with people who had come to hear this child prodigy play for them. Yo-Yo did not disappoint them. The reviews of the recital were outstanding. Critic Allen Hughes of the *New York Times* wrote, "The cello recital he gave at Carnegie Recital Hall Thursday night was of a quality to make many an older man green with envy."

Strong reviews like this one were very important to a young musician like Yo-Yo. They helped him build a career. His mother often went out to the newsstands early in the morning just after the New York papers came out to look for the reviews of Yo-Yo's performance the night before. Together, Yo-Yo and his mother would read the review, holding their breath and hoping that it would praise his performance. They were rarely disappointed.

THE TRIALS OF A TEENAGER

Not only was Yo-Yo a brilliant young cellist; he was also a very bright student. He attended high school at Professional Children's School, a private school in New York City. He was so much smarter than most other students, though, that he easily became bored and distracted. From time to time, he would not show up at his classes and would simply wander around New York. This gave him time alone to think. Fortunately, the school eventually put him into an accelerated program that enabled him to graduate from high school in 1970, at age 15.

Yo-Yo then began to attend classes on a part-time basis at the college division of the Julliard School, one of the world's foremost music conservatories. At Julliard, gifted musicians study music and take courses in the business of managing their musical careers. A few become world-famous soloists, but many others fill positions in symphony orchestras across the United States. Yo-Yo attended Julliard while he also continued to work with Leonard Rose.

During the summer of 1970, he attended the Meadowmount School of Music, in upstate New York. Founded in 1944 by Russian violinist Ivan Galamian, the camp was the first of its kind for young musicians. For Yo-Yo, his summer at Meadowmount was the first time that he had been on his own, away from home. Away from his father's watchful eye and strict discipline, Yo-Yo began to change. He experienced a rebellion against the rigid guidelines that had governed his life as a young musician.

For the first time, Yo-Yo did not practice on a strict schedule. On more than one occasion, he lost his cello. As he recalled, "I would leave my cello outside, not worrying if it might rain, and run off to play Ping-Pong." He also "took some white paint and decorated the stone walls with graffiti. . . ." Nevertheless, Yo-Yo continued to perform brilliantly, even without much practice and with time out to paint graffiti. One student who attended Meadowmount recalled that his performances were "appassionato ["very passionate"], full of abandon, tremendously impressive."

After the summer, Yo-Yo returned to New York. His hair was longer, he wore a leather jacket, and he had begun to swear, even in the presence of Leonard Rose. "I'm embarrassed when I think of the language I used," he said. "But Mr. Rose took it in stride and saw me through this phase. At some level, he must have been very happy to find me opening up in that way. And, for some reason, he kept his faith in me."

In 1971, Yo-Yo applied to Columbia University in New York, which accepted him. He continued to live at home and practice while trying to take college courses. It was too much pressure for a boy of 16, though, and he left after one semester. Yo-Yo was upset with himself for dropping out, and he did not tell his parents, who assumed that he was still attending classes.

Instead, Yo-Yo went back to Julliard, where he practiced. He also met other students who were older than he was and tried to gain their acceptance. Yo-Yo obtained a false identification (ID) card and began to drink alcohol. Unfortunately, he was totally inexperienced with drinking. One Friday afternoon, he was supposed to work with his father and mother during a rehearsal of the Children's Orchestra. Yo-Yo never made it to rehearsal. During the session, Marina received a telephone call from someone at Julliard who told her that Yo-Yo had been rushed off to the emergency department of a nearby hospital. He had passed out from too much drinking. Marina Ma rushed to the hospital and found her son recovering from the incident. She immediately spoke to the doctor who was treating Yo-Yo; he assured her that Yo-Yo would be fine.

Although this was the first serious incident in Yo-Yo's life, it was much greater than a single instance of too much drinking. Marina realized that Yo-Yo's father would be very upset when he found out what had happened. In Chinese families, a mistake committed by a child reflects badly on his parents. Dr. Ma

Yo-Yo Ma would return to the site of his triumphant 1971 recital. In 1991, he played Bach's cello suites again at Carnegie Hall.

would also be angry that Yo-Yo was not attending Columbia and was wasting time drinking when he should have been practicing the cello to advance his career.

When Dr. Ma spoke with Yo-Yo, however, he did not become angry. Instead, he emphasized his son's lack of responsibility in not meeting his commitments to practice with the Children's Orchestra. There was "deep shame in the Ma household," Yo-Yo said. In addition, Dr. Ma blamed himself for what had happened. He thought that Yo-Yo might have begun to drink because he saw his father enjoy a glass of wine with dinner. In the future, Dr. Ma resolved not to drink any wine.

With this incident, the crisis of Yo-Yo's adolescence seemed to pass. He now faced an important decision in his life. Columbia had not been to his liking. He needed to decide what the next stage of his education would be. He could attend Julliard full time for a conservatory education, or he could opt for a broader education at a liberal arts college. Yo-Yo was interested in Harvard University, near his sister's school in Boston. He felt that a broad liberal arts education would enable him to take courses in subjects such as history and philosophy. These would deepen his understanding of the historical periods in which classical composers lived and broaden his knowledge of the events and ideas that influenced their music. As a result of his decision to attend Harvard, Yo-Yo would bring much, much more to his own performances as a classical cellist.

5

Success as a Young Cellist

Recalling Yo-Yo Ma's decision to go to Harvard, Isaac Stern said, "Yo-Yo made a decision rather remarkable for a talented young man of his age, and that was to try to get an education. He could have devoted all his time to preparing pieces for concerts and competitions, but he took the unusual step of deciding to become a person."

Yo-Yo Ma entered Harvard in 1972 and majored in humanities, not music. His courses included world history; fine art courses in which he learned about painting; astronomy courses in which he studied the galaxies; sociology courses that helped him understand how societies operate; and European literature courses in which he studied the works of Russian, German, and French authors. Yo-Yo had a wide-ranging curiosity that took him in many different directions and exposed him to all types of learning.

Unlike his approach to music, however, he did not strive for perfection in his courses. Ma was content with above-average grades. Sometimes he would leave a paper or the preparation for an important exam until the last minute, then study late into the night. By his own admission, he did not apply self-discipline in many of his studies. Yo-Yo was still experiencing the adolescent rebellion that had overtaken him in New York and at Meadowmount.

While he pursued his liberal arts studies, Yo-Yo Ma also continued to play music. He was in constant demand to give recitals. He knew that too many concerts, however, would interfere with his coursework at Harvard. Therefore, he accepted only one concert date per month. In the meantime, he tried to learn and improve his own skills through the people he met and those with whom he played.

One of these people was Leon Kirchner, a composer and Harvard professor who taught chamber music. Leon Kirchner was born in Brooklyn in 1919, then moved with his parents to California, where he attended the University of California at Berkeley. He soon became a gifted pianist and later an orchestra conductor. Kirchner also spent much of his time composing pieces for full orchestra as well as chamber music for smaller groups. Chamber music is generally played with a few instruments, such as violin, cello, and piano. In 1953, Kirchner won the prestigious Naumburg Award for his Concerto for Piano no. 1. A concerto is a piece for a solo instrument, such as a piano or violin, and an orchestra. In 1966, Kirchner won the Pulitzer Prize in music for his String Quartet no. 3. Many orchestras asked him to compose works especially for their musicians. These have included the New York Philharmonic, the Philadelphia Orchestra, and the Boston Symphony Orchestra. In 1992, Kirchner was awarded the prestigious Friedman Award for his Music for Cello and Orchestra. For 30 years, from 1961 to 1991, he was Professor of Music at Harvard.

Kirchner was not the only person who had a major impact on Yo-Yo Ma's life. Another person who also influenced Ma was the pianist Luise Vosgerchian, who played with the Boston Symphony Orchestra. According to Ma, Vosgerchian helped

Pulitzer Prize–winning composer Leon Kirchner, seen here playing piano, had a major impact of Yo-Yo Ma's life at Harvard.

him to interpret a musical piece in his own way. Another superb pianist, Patricia Zander, encouraged him to take greater risks in his playing and stretch his limits so he could play to his full potential.

Under the influence of his playing partners and Professor Kirchner, Yo-Yo Ma continued to grow as a cellist. As John Attanas wrote, "Kirchner was a strong-willed teacher who had no problem criticizing his students. He quickly discovered how talented Yo-Yo was. But his discovery did not dissuade him from criticizing Ma. In fact, Yo-Yo's huge talent turned Kirchner into an even harsher critic."

While he was at Harvard, Yo-Yo Ma also began to perform with two other students, Richard Kogan and Lynn Chang. He had met both of them at Julliard in New York. Kogan is a pianist who later went on to medical school and became a psychiatrist. Chang is a gifted violinist who, along with Yo-Yo Ma, was enrolled in Professor Kirchner's class. The three students practiced for many hours before performing their pieces to audiences at Harvard. Yo-Yo Ma also appeared in solo performances of compositions such as the Bach suites. He was so well known on the Harvard campus that his concerts were sold out.

MORE CONCERTS

As *New York Times* reporter Leslie Rubinstein wrote, "Yo-Yo Ma is one Asian soloist who could never be accused of repressing his feelings in a stereotypically Oriental way. His slender face, framed by thin wire glasses, has an open spiritual quality." According to Yo-Yo Ma, "My parents taught me to believe in the soul, that something extra which in Chinese is called *ling,* the beautiful part of human nature." At times, though, Ma felt that he had trouble reaching his soul because his playing was so restricted by self-discipline and the desire for perfection. This made taking risks, stretching boundaries, and playing with more emotion difficult because of the possibility of making mistakes.

Much of the pressure that Yo-Yo Ma felt came from his parents and their experience during World War II. "The demand for perfection, all that pressure, came from the wars. My parents

A 1976 graduate of Harvard University, Yo-Yo Ma performed at his alma mater in 2004 before receiving the tenth annual Harvard Arts Medal.

had anguished lives. They saw antiques chopped up for fuel, all sorts of violence, and that left them with the sense that all that lasts are skills." In 1974, Yo-Yo Ma was preparing to deliver a concert in New York City. He practiced pieces by nineteenth-century German composers Franz Schubert, Johannes Brahms, and Robert Schumann. Yo-Yo Ma performed at the 92nd Street Y (short for the Young Men's and Young Women's Hebrew

Between the Generations

CHINESE IMMIGRANTS IN AMERICA

The wildly enthusiastic reception that musicians like Yo-Yo Ma and Lynn Chang received at Harvard was a relatively new experience for Chinese Americans. Chinese immigrants began to appear in the United States during the early 1850s. They came to California, where gold had been discovered in 1849. Some of them became miners, but many others opened small businesses that served the prospectors working in the gold fields. These businesses included restaurants and laundries. Often they had no other choice. The Chinese faced discrimination in the gold fields, where they were forced out by white miners. After the gold rush ended, many Chinese went to work on the railroads. They helped lay the tracks for a transcontinental railroad, which was completed in 1869. Although they were paid very low wages, the Chinese worked long hours, laying as much as 10 miles of track in a single day. Many of the immigrants lived in a Chinese neighborhood (called Chinatown) of cities like San Francisco. There they faced discrimination and were not permitted to become U.S. citizens. During the 1870s, discrimination against Chinese immigrants increased. The U.S. economy fell into a depression, jobs were scarce, and white employees blamed Chinese immigrants for taking work away from them. Protests against Chinese immigration broke out in U.S. cities. In 1882, Congress passed the Chinese Exclusion Act, cutting off most Chinese immigration. This law remained in effect until the

Association), a popular location for lectures and classical music in uptown New York.

"I practiced for a year because I wanted to give a perfect New York recital," he said. The seats were filled, and at the end of the concert, the audience applauded wildly. *New York Times* music critic Donal Henahan wrote, "The difference between playing a piece of music and performing it is vast, and probably cannot

1940s, when it was finally repealed. Chinese immigration began to increase. Finally, in the 1950s, Chinese immigrants were permitted to become American citizens.

During the 1960s and 1970s, the number of Chinese immigrants to the United States continued to grow. Many of these immigrants were like the Ma family. Indeed, Chinese concert musicians like Yo-Yo Ma became well known across America. Isaac Stern called Ma "the greatest cellist alive." By the late 1970s, at least 10 Chinese students were in a concert at the Julliard School, whereas several years earlier there would have been few, if any.

In the last quarter of the twentieth century, Chinese musicians were coming to the United States in greater numbers and for a variety of reasons. Among these reasons was the number of orchestras in which gifted musicians could find jobs. In addition, changes in U.S. laws made immigration far easier. Finally, the freedom that immigrants found in the United States enabled them to express themselves more openly. This situation was in marked contrast to the authoritarian government in Communist China. As Yo-Yo Ma himself recalled, his father told him that "boys don't cry. I knew they did, because I wept constantly at what was beautiful." In the United States, Yo-Yo learned to play with greater abandon. As he threw back his head and drew his bow across the cello, he could express emotion through his music and play memorable performances.

be taught. One of the 'performers,' and already a major one at age 19, is Yo-Yo Ma, who gave an extraordinary recital. . . ." As Yo-Yo Ma completed the concert, however, he was not happy with himself. "I was bored. I could have walked out. After that, I decided I couldn't live that way. I must be vitally interested at every moment."

One way that Ma kept himself interested was through a wide range of studies at Harvard. Part of Chinese culture is a love of study and learning—a love that Ma inherited. Instead of simply mastering the cello section of a piece of music that might be designed for a chamber group or an orchestra, he tried to understand the entire composition.

> While I was at Harvard, I gained a new vocabulary for understanding music. . . . I was fascinated to realize how a composer can create interest in his musical line by varying the lengths of phrases. Bach, for instance, may write several successive phrases of uneven length . . . which provide a lot of surprises. . . . The interpreter [the musician] always has to be aware of questions of shape and structure. It takes much experience to be able to sustain the listener's attention over a span of twenty or thirty minutes.

LOVE IN MARLBORO

One place that Yo-Yo Ma honed his skills was at the Marlboro Music School and Festival in Marlboro, Vermont. He began to attend the school before entering Harvard. Indeed, he was fortunate enough to play in an orchestra there directed by Pablo Casals. At Marlboro, founded in 1951, music students are taught by the masters and play together with them at the annual music festival each summer. During his first summer at Marlboro, Ma met a young woman named Jill Hornor, from Mount Holyoke

Cellist Pablo Casals conducts an orchestra in a Marlboro Music Festival performance. Yo-Yo Ma attended the music festival before entering Harvard.

College, in Massachusetts. She was working in the administration building at the music school.

Ma was attracted to Jill, but at first he was too shy to say anything to her. By summer's end, however, he told her that he was in love with her. At first Jill Horner did not believe him. She went to Paris to study for her junior year, and Yo-Yo Ma entered Harvard. He persisted, however, and continued to write to her. An exchange of letters as well as telephone calls soon began. Jill Horner came back to the United States and graduated from Mt. Holyoke. Then she went to Cornell University in Ithaca, New York, for graduate studies in German. By this time, Yo-Yo Ma's love for her had deepened to the point where he wanted to marry her.

There were problems, however. Ma knew that his parents would be upset that he had not chosen a Chinese woman to marry. They would be fearful that a Westerner might not carry on the Chinese traditions when she and Ma had children. In addition, he was not sure how Hornor would react to a proposal of marriage.

Nevertheless, in 1977 he decided that the time to find out had come. Yo-Yo Ma bought an engagement ring and traveled to Ithaca. Outside Jill's apartment, he telephoned her to make sure she was at home. Several minutes later, he showed up at her front door and asked her to marry him. She accepted immediately. The couple then flew to Cleveland, Ohio, to tell Hornor's parents. They were happy to accept a new son-in-law, but with Ma's parents, it was a different story. They were not very pleased about the engagement.

Jill Hornor and Yo-Yo Ma were married later in 1977. At first, the closeness between Ma and his parents disappeared. After a few years, though, during the early 1980s, Ma and his wife had two children. They were given Chinese names as well as American names—Nicholas and Emily. Gradually, through the grandchildren, Yo-Yo Ma and his parents rebuilt their relationship.

6

Young Cellist on Tour

Yo-Yo Ma's first job after college kept him at Harvard. The university appointed him as artist-in-residence. This meant that he was expected to teach students who were trying to master the cello, as well as to play concerts on campus. Ma's fame as a cellist also brought him many concert dates outside Harvard.

In January 1977, for example, Ma returned to the 92nd Street Y for a recital in front of a packed house. One of his selections was a piece written by Polish-born composer Frederic Chopin. A gifted pianist, Chopin wrote most of his works for the piano. This piece, though, had been specially arranged by Ma's teacher, Leonard Rose, to be played on the cello. In addition, Ma played a piece by twentieth-century composer David Popper. Music critic John Rockwell of the *New York Times* called Ma's recital "about as dazzling a piece of technical flamboyance on the cello as this listener has ever heard."

In addition, Ma played one of the Bach cello suites and a piece by German composer Johannes Brahms. Rockwell added, "Mr. Ma played everything with intelligence and style." He

JOHANNES BRAHMS (1833–1897)

Born in Hamburg, Germany, Brahms was taught to play the piano by his father, Jakob. The elder Brahms was a horn player, who performed with local bands in Hamburg. Johannes also received piano lessons from music teachers who helped him improve his skills. As a teenager, Brahms played the piano in restaurants along the waterfront to help support his family. Meanwhile, he had begun to compose music. During the 1850s, Brahms was introduced to prominent composer Robert Schumann and his wife, Clara. The Schumanns recognized Brahms's unique talents as a composer and helped him achieve recognition for his music. Schumann died in 1856, after years of battling mental illness, and Brahms retained a close relationship with Clara. Although Clara Schumann was in love with Brahms, he seemed uninterested in marriage, so the couple never married. In fact, Brahms remained a bachelor for his entire life. As he once said, "I couldn't bear to have in the house a woman who has the right to be kind to me, to comfort me when things go wrong."

During the latter part of the 1850s, Brahms supported himself by teaching piano and conducting a choir. Meanwhile, he continued to compose music, including his Piano Concerto no. 1 (1854–1858). In 1863, Brahms moved to Vienna, Austria, a center of classical music during the nineteenth century. There he became director of the Vienna Philharmonic Orchestra, one of the leading orchestras in Europe. By the 1870s, he had become famous across Europe for his chamber music and his symphonies. In fact, he was considered among the leading composers of the era, along with Wolfgang Amadeus Mozart and Ludwig van Beethoven. Brahms was also influenced by gypsy music played in Europe, and composed a series of Hungarian Dances based on gypsy songs. Among his later works was a sonata for violin, arranged for cello by Leonard Rose and played by Yo-Yo Ma.

described Ma's emotional performance as filled with "tortured, soulful grimaces." Although applauding him for his excellent playing, Rockwell added, that "he hasn't yet reached the level of simple musical conviction that the great masters of the instrument have attained. But no doubt he'll get there, and in the meantime the sounds he makes are almost enough."

Yo-Yo Ma was constantly pushing himself to perform with greater perfection and to achieve deeper insight into his music. During the time he spent at Harvard, his skills continued to improve. In April 1978, he returned to the 92nd Street Y for another recital. Joseph Horowitz of the *New York Times* applauded his performance, calling him a "cellist of staggering ability" whose "technical resources are extraordinary."

That year, Yo-Yo Ma won the prestigious Avery Fisher Prize. Fisher was the founder of an electronics firm specializing in stereo equipment. A wealthy philanthropist, Fisher financed a music hall at Lincoln Center in New York. Called Avery Fisher Hall, it is an important center of classical music. In the past, the Fisher Prize had been given to multiple musicians. Yo-Yo Ma was the first solo winner of the prize. He entered the competition and was selected by a committee of outstanding musicians and music educators who listened to a number of performances by gifted artists before awarding the prize to Ma. He was also awarded a cash prize of $2,500.

ON TOUR

In the field of classical music, a prestigious award like the Fisher Prize is a performer's ticket to stardom. After winning the prize, Ma was asked to perform with orchestras in New York and in other cities across the United States. In addition, he was signed by major recording companies to record classical music albums. Later in 1978, Ma appeared in New York at the Mostly Mozart Festival. This was a popular series of concerts staged during the summer that attracted huge crowds. The concerts featured the music of eighteenth-century composer Wolfgang Amadeus Mozart, as well as other classical composers.

Yo-Yo Ma appeared in a trio that included pianist Peter Serkin and violinist Alexander Schneider. They played music by Mozart and Beethoven. Describing Ma's playing of the

WOLFGANG AMADEUS MOZART (1756–1791)

Born in Salzburg, Austria, Mozart was a child prodigy. He learned to play the violin and harpsichord (similar to a piano) from his father, Leopold Mozart. Leopold Mozart took his son as well as his daughter, Maria Anna, to various courts in central Europe to perform for the nobility, including the empress of Austria. Young Wolfgang was considered among the greatest performers of his generation. Meanwhile, Mozart had already begun to compose music. During the 1760s and 1770s, he wrote symphonies, operas, and quartets. In addition, Mozart composed violin concertos, six piano sonatas, and a piano concerto. He continued to live in Salzburg during the mid 1770s, supporting himself as concertmaster at the court of the local prince. In 1777, he left Salzburg and traveled to Paris, capital of France. Paris was a major city that seemed to offer much larger audiences for Mozart's music and greater recognition for his unusual talents. He did not succeed in finding a position to support himself, however, and returned to Salzburg.

In 1780, Mozart traveled to Munich, Germany, to compose an opera, and from there he went to Vienna, the capital of Austria. A major center for classical music, Vienna became Mozart's home until his death. He composed a series of piano concertos as well as operas, quartets, sonatas, and quintets. Mozart supported himself by publishing his music, playing in various orchestras, teaching students, and composing small pieces of music commissioned by local nobles for their parties. He died at age 35 of a mysterious fever, leaving some of his important musical compositions incomplete.

In the year that Yo-Yo Ma was awarded the Avery Fisher Prize, he also made four appearances during the opening week of the thirteenth annual Mostly Mozart Festival at Avery Fisher Hall.

Beethoven piece, Harold Schonberg, music critic for the *New York Times*, wrote, "Mr. Ma played the work with perfect control. His armament is formidable; there seems nothing in finger or bow that gives him any problems."

As a result of his concert schedule, Yo-Yo Ma spent many days away from home. He admitted his busy life had changed the type of marriage that he had hoped to have with his wife. "We had visions of an equal relationship where we would share the cooking, share taking out the garbage—share everything. To make matters worse, I've proved horrible at all domestic chores." At first, he added, the concert schedule "seemed terribly exciting." Then he found himself with "as many as a hundred and fifty concerts a season. I was always flirting with getting burned out from exhaustion."

Early in 1979, Ma was back at the 92nd Street Y for a concert with violinist Lynn Chang and pianist Richard Kogan. Chang had just won the Young Concert Artists award, and the concert was designed to celebrate his outstanding achievement.

LUDWIG VAN BEETHOVEN (1770–1827)

Born in Bonn, Germany, Beethoven is considered possibly the greatest composer in the history of music. Much of his music is filled with great emotional power—a characteristic of the so-called Romantic Age of art and culture during the nineteenth century. During the 1780s, Beethoven became a student of Christian Gottlob Neefe, the organist at the court of Prince Maximilian Francis in Bonn. Beethoven was so talented that, in 1782, he was appointed Neefe's assistant at court. Beethoven continued to work in Bonn during the 1780s, playing in the local theater and teaching music to the children of well-to-do parents. He also gained a wide reputation as an outstanding pianist. During the same period, Beethoven was writing pieces of music, including several piano sonatas. Some of his work was read by famed composer Franz Joseph Haydn, who asked Beethoven to come to Vienna as his student. In 1795, Beethoven performed one of his own compositions, a piano concerto, for a large audience in Vienna. He continued to present new works over the next five years, including his First Symphony in 1800.

The performers played a trio by Johannes Brahms. As Allen Hughes of the *Times* wrote, "The sound of a bow hitting a string was never heard. . . . Instead, it was a matter of lovingly phrased, pensive melody, finely balanced violin-cello duets, muted, mysterious dialogues between cello and piano . . . such beautiful playing that their virtuosity could not be doubted. . . ."

In July, Yo-Yo Ma returned to the Mostly Mozart Festival, at which he played one of Bach's suites for cello. He "gave a completely involving performance," one reporter wrote. "Mr. Ma has an uncommon ability to pick out the right note to emphasize. . .a chord, so that Bach's melodic lines stand out." In December, Ma played once again at Lincoln Center. His performances included pieces by Brahms and the French composer Maurice Ravel.

By the early nineteenth century, Beethoven was growing increasingly deaf. For a composer and musician, no problem could have been much more serious. Beethoven considered suicide. "But only Art held back," he said, "for, ah, it seemed unthinkable for me to leave the world forever before I had produced all that I felt called upon to produce." Then he vowed to continue. "I will seize fate by the throat. If only I were rid of my affliction I would embrace the whole world." By 1819, Beethoven was completely deaf, yet he continued to produce great music. These works included the Fifth Symphony, written in 1808, the Seventh and Eighth symphonies written in 1811–1812, and the Ninth Symphony written in 1824. To present his Ninth Symphony, Beethoven conducted the orchestra himself. When the audience stood to applaud the symphony, which combines instrumental with choral music, Beethoven could not hear them. Finally, he turned from conducting to face the rest of the concert hall and recognized that his symphony had been a tremendous success. As a result of Beethoven's work, instrumental music, which had taken second place to choral music in the past, was considered its equal by composers and audiences across Europe.

Born in eastern France in 1875, Ravel was trained at the Paris Conservatoire. This was a prestigious center of music education, where Ravel stayed from 1889 until 1905. In his early period, while still a young man, Ravel composed one of his most famous pieces, *Pavane for a Dead Princess*. A pavane is a dance that was popular in European courts. Many of Ravel's works were composed for solo piano. In addition, he wrote string quartets and a trio for violin, cello, and piano, which was composed in 1914. After three years in the French Army during World War I, Ravel continued to compose music, including a sonata for violin and cello. This work was performed by Yo-Yo Ma at Lincoln Center in December 1979.

CLASSICAL RECORDINGS

While he was on tour, Yo-Yo Ma also took time out to make classical recordings. In 1979, for example, he recorded a concerto by Ludwig van Beethoven for the large German recording company Deutsche Grammophon. Ma played with a young German violinist, Anne-Sophie Mutter. A review of the recording in 1980 called Ma's work "incredible." Mutter's performance on the violin was equally impressive.

Born in Baden, Germany, in 1963, Anne-Sophie Mutter was a child prodigy on the violin. She was awarded numerous prizes while still a child and left school to play violin full time. At age 13, she was a soloist with the Berlin Philharmonic, one of the world's most famous orchestras. A year later, she appeared with the English Chamber Orchestra in a concert at the Salzburg Music Festival in Austria. This annual festival is considered one of the premier events in classical music. Mutter recorded violin pieces by Mozart when she was only 15 and joined Yo-Yo Ma the following year. In 1980, Mutter came to the United States, where she has continued a career as one of the world's great violinists. Mutter won Grammy Awards in 1994, 1999, 2000, and 2005.

After his work with Anne-Sophie Mutter, Yo-Yo Ma went on to record two cello concertos by German composer Franz Joseph Haydn. This work was recorded for CBS Records, with whom Ma had signed a contract. CBS was a major record producer, and only the best-known classical musicians were asked to record for the company. Commenting on Ma's recordings, one critic wrote, "With his brilliant technique, finely tuned silken tone and cultured musical instincts, Yo-Yo Ma is the perfect interpreter" of the Haydn cello concertos.

PERSONAL CRISIS

While Yo-Yo Ma's work continued, he suffered a personal crisis that almost ended his career. Ma suffered from a condition called scoliosis. This is a curvature of the spine. In a cello player, such as Ma, the curvature can become a very serious problem because he must bend over his instrument to play it. The doctors who diagnosed the illness feared that it could grow worse unless Ma underwent an operation. Indeed, without surgery, the worsening condition could affect the nerves in Ma's spine and make playing the cello impossible. They recommended an immediate operation. The surgery itself was risky, however, and Ma might never recover fully enough to play the cello again.

In April 1980, Ma underwent the operation, which was performed by an orthopedic surgeon named John Hall. Steel rods were inserted into Ma's back to stretch his spine. After the operation, he was placed in an upper body cast to give his spine time to heal. While he was in the hospital, his wife visited him often and brought his cello. Holes were cut in the cast for Ma's arms so he could practice. Fortunately, he fully recovered from the surgery, growing two inches taller after his spine was straightened out. "It gave me time to think," he said. "I'm always trying to understand life itself through my music making, searching for a different way to tell the truth."

FRANZ JOSEPH HAYDN (1732–1809)

Born in Austria, Haydn was the son of Matthias Haydn—mayor of the village of Rohrau and a harp player. When he was only five years old, young Franz Joseph was sent to live with a relative who conducted a choir in a nearby city. After singing there for a couple of years and playing various instruments, he was invited to become part of the choir at St. Stephen's Cathedral in Vienna. He remained there for nine years, until he lost his high voice and was dismissed from the choir. Meanwhile, Haydn had begun to compose music. He soon obtained a new position from Karl Joseph von Furnberg, a wealthy Austrian, for whom Haydn composed string quartets. His success there led to an even more prestigious position—music director and composer for Count Ferdinand Maximilian von Morzin. He conducted the orchestra and wrote various compositions, including a symphony.

In 1761, after a short stay with von Morzin, Haydn was invited to become the assistant music director for Prince Anton Esterhazy, one of the most prominent men in the Austrian empire. Between 1761 and 1765, Haydn composed his First Cello Concerto. By 1766, he had become Esterhazy's music director. Haydn remained at the court of Prince Esterhazy for almost 30 years. He earned a comfortable salary and composed symphonies, string quartets, and operas. In 1784, he composed another cello concerto. The music was lost and not rediscovered until 1961. In nearby Vienna, Haydn met Wolfgang Amadeus Mozart, and the two composers became good friends. In 1790, Prince Esterhazy died, and his son was not a music lover. Haydn left the court and traveled to England, where he composed 12 symphonies. Haydn later moved to Vienna.

During his lifetime, he had written many symphonies and string quartets, greatly expanding these two forms of music across Europe. As Mozart once said, Haydn "alone has the secret of making me smile and touching me at the bottom of my soul. There is no one who can do it all—to joke and terrify, to evoke laughter and profound sentiment—and all equally well: except Joseph Haydn."

When Yo-Yo Ma realized that there was a chance he might never play again, he had to confront the possibility of a life without performing. He told himself that he could take up another type of work, like teaching. After he was informed that the operation had been a success, though, Ma realized how important a role performing classical music played in his life. As he said, "I'm really happy to be a cellist."

After the operation, Yo-Yo Ma continued to perform. In some of his performances, he appeared with the classical pianist Emmanuel Ax. Born in Lvov, Poland, in 1950, Ax came to the United States with his parents when he was still a child. Later he was accepted to the Julliard School, where he played as accompanist to cello teacher Leonard Rose. Through Rose, Ax met Yo-Yo Ma. After first hearing Ma play the cello, Ax said, "I was completely bowled over. It seemed like the most perfect playing I'd ever heard." The two musicians played together briefly in 1971, then lost touch for a while. In the meantime, Ax won a prestigious piano competition in 1974 and was booked to play with many orchestras. Eventually, the two busy performers had time to renew their friendship and began to play together again in 1979.

In 1980, they appeared together at Lincoln Center. They played a sonata written by Brahms for piano and violin but arranged by Ma for the cello. Music critic Donal Henahan wrote that "Mr. Ma's cello . . . sang out its part richly and easily." In addition, they played a Beethoven sonata. "In the Beethoven sonata," wrote Henahan, "the two young virtuosos [outstanding musicians] struck sparks right from the start, and the result was a brilliant performance of one of the most difficult works in the literature."

In 1982, Ma and Ax appeared together again. This time they played a concert at the Metropolitan Museum of Art in New York City, which featured pieces by Brahms and Beethoven. As reporter Tim Page noted, "Mr. Ma is the consummate extrovert,

Yo-Yo Ma began playing with pianist Emanuel Ax (*center*) in 1979. Here he shares a laugh with Ax as Peter Ustinov delivers a comedic musical tribute to violinist Isaac Stern during an eightieth birthday concert for Stern at Carnegie Hall.

inclined to the demonstrative on-stage," in his playing. "Mr. Ax, on the other hand is more steady and reserved. . . . The two men obviously enjoy working with each other, and they were warmly received by an overflow crowd." Indeed, both men had developed a close personal relationship not only on stage but also in their lives away from music.

Yo-Yo Ma's own personal appearances continued to follow a rather hectic schedule. In 1981, he played in a summer music festival at Caramoor, an estate located in Katonah, New York. This is one of the leading summer music festivals in the United States. In 1982, he also appeared at Lincoln Center, playing two of Bach's cello suites. Edward Rothstein of the *New York Times* called his performances "simple and elegant." That same year,

Ma also recorded an acclaimed album with Emmanuel Ax, playing sonatas by Beethoven.

As the praise for Yo-Yo Ma's performances continued, he began to approach a position reserved for very few classical musicians—superstardom.

7

Becoming a Classical Superstar

In 1985, Yo-Yo Ma received a Grammy Award for his recording of Bach's cello suites. The Grammy, the most prestigious award in music, is given to performers and composers in a variety of musical categories, including classical, rock and roll, jazz, and country. Winning the Grammy distinguishes a performer from his or her peers as someone special and unusually talented. Many performers are happy to win the Grammy once.

Ma not only received the Grammy in 1984. He won two more awards for recordings released the following year. These included the cello sonatas of Johannes Brahms and another recording that featured cello concertos by British composers Edward Elgar and William Walton. In 1986, Yo-Yo Ma and Emmanuel Ax released a recording of a Beethoven cello sonata, which was also awarded a Grammy. Over the next several years, Yo-Yo Ma won additional Grammy Awards. He received these honors for other classical music recordings, which included cello works by English composer Benjamin

Britten, American composer Samuel Barber, Johannes Brahms, and Russian composer Pyotr Ilyich Tchaikovsky.

A HECTIC MUSICAL LIFE

Yo-Yo Ma's multiple awards had lifted him into the ranks of a classical superstar. Very few performers ever reach this pinnacle of success. He continued to record and maintained a hectic touring schedule. One tour took him across the West to San Francisco, Los Angeles, Portland, and Seattle. In 1986, he traveled to China, his parents' homeland, and then returned for another concert tour there the following year. In an interview with author David Blum, Ma recalled that he was nearly burning out from the hectic pace of his tours. It had been one thing to keep up this pace before he and Jill had children. After his son was born, however, Ma resolved to spend more time with his family. He admitted that his model was the classical violinist Itzhak Perlman. A child prodigy like Yo-Yo Ma, the Israeli-born Pearlman is also a classical superstar:

> Itzhak Perlman, who is dedicated to his family, showed me how to take a good, hard look at a schedule and protect time for my family. I reserve the dates of the kids' birthdays, and keep the month of July exclusively for the family. I'm taking more short respites [breaks] from touring, and learning not to get as hyped up as before. Finally, I decided that it's not enough just to make time to be at home; I have to preserve the quality of that time. So, aside from practicing, I don't let professional obligations encroach upon my family life.

Yo-Yo Ma also tried to find time to visit his parents. During the 1980s, Ma's parents lived in New York and in Taiwan, an island off the coast of China. Because the Chinese Communists controlled China, Dr. Ma could not return to his homeland.

Isaac Stern (*center*) answers questions as other musicians look on during a joint news conference in Tokyo, Japan, in 1986. From left are Yo-Yo Ma, violinist Jaime Laredo, Stern, Chinese violinist Lian Lin, and American composer Mark Peskanov.

Nevertheless, he and his wife went to Taiwan, where Chiang Kai-shek had fled in 1949. Since that time, Chiang and his successors governed Taiwan. Dr. Ma's health gradually grew worse during the late 1980s. When Yo-Yo Ma's parents were in New York, Ma visited his father regularly and played for him. Dr. Ma died in 1991.

CROSSOVER MUSIC

Although Yo-Yo Ma continued to play classical concerts, he also began to explore other types of music. One reason was that the number of classical pieces featuring the cello was quite limited.

Classical composers wrote far more music designed to feature the piano or violin. These include piano and violin concertos, sonatas, and other pieces. With a limited number of cello pieces to master and perform, a supertalent like Ma could easily become bored. A second reason was that classical music does not have as large an audience as rock-and-roll or country music. As a result, recording companies encouraged their performers like Yo-Yo Ma to explore other forms of music that might be more popular. Ma had signed agreements with CBS Records and later Sony. These companies wanted their recording stars to cross over—that is, try music that combined classical with jazz, country, or some other type of music.

In addition, Yo-Yo Ma was not only interested in classical music. He was eager to learn how to play other forms of music, such as jazz and country. Ma sees all forms of music as being related to each other. Playing different types of music simply enables him to become a better musician. It also means that he can reach more people and enrich their lives with his music. Ma possesses a never-ending desire to work with other performers in different musical fields and to improve his own skills by listening to them. Even after becoming a superstar, Yo-Yo Ma never developed a large ego. His humility has enabled him to be taught by other musicians and to play with them without having to be the star of the show himself.

During the last quarter of the twentieth century, one of the best-known jazz composers and musicians was French pianist Claude Bolling. Born in 1930 in Cannes, on the French Mediterranean coast, Bolling played in French nightclubs and made recordings with American jazz musicians. During the 1970s, he composed a Suite for Flute and Jazz Piano Trio that became very popular. The music featured a famous classical flutist, French virtuoso Jean-Pierre Rampal. Because of the suite's success, Bolling composed and recorded other suites for jazz and classical performers.

Bolling's works were considered crossover music. They combined jazz with classical sounds. In 1984, Bolling recorded a Suite for Cello and Jazz Piano Trio, featuring Yo-Yo Ma. The music combined slow, sentimental sections with faster movements. These provided Ma with an opportunity to perform jazz pieces with a fine trio. It was his first venture into crossover music, but not his last.

SAMUEL BARBER (1910–1981), BENJAMIN BRITTEN (1913–1976), AND PYOTR ILYICH TCHAIKOVSKY (1840–1893)

Among Ma's favorite composers are Samuel Barber, Benjamin Britten, and Pytor Tchaikovsky. Born in Pennsylvania, Samuel Barber was trained at the Curtis Institute of Music in Philadelphia. He enrolled in a wide range of courses, including piano, composing, and conducting. During the 1930s, he composed a musical overture, or introduction, to a play called *The School for Scandal*, written during the eighteenth century. In addition, he wrote a string quartet in 1936, and a slow movement from this work became widely popular as the "Adagio for Strings." Barber also wrote a violin concerto and a cello concerto during the 1940s as well as music designed for orchestra and chorus. In 1963, he was awarded the Pulitzer Prize in music for his piano concerto.

Born in England, Benjamin Britten was strongly influenced by his mother, a singer. As a child, he had already begun to write music early in the morning before attending school. In 1930, Britten began to attend the Royal College of Music, where he studied piano and composing. During the 1930s, he wrote music for films but soon expanded his repertoire to other types of compositions. These included choral music, *Hymn to Saint Cecilia* and *A Ceremony of Carols*, written in the 1940s. He also wrote several operas, including *Peter Grimes* and *Billy Budd*, the latter based on a story by American author Herman Melville. In addition, Britten produced cello suites and a cello symphony. He also wrote

Three years later, Ma went to a well-known jazz club in New York, the Blue Note, to listen to French jazz violinist Stéphane Grappelli. Born in 1908, Grappelli learned how to play the piano and violin when he was very young. During the 1920s, he performed in Parisian dance bands and later appeared with jazz combos in night clubs. As his popularity grew, he began to tour western Europe and the United States. In 1988, Ma was asked

a choral work called *War Requiem,* completed in 1961. One critic called it "Britten's masterpiece."

Pyotr Tchaikovsky was born in Votkinsk, Russia, the son of a local factory manager. Tchaikovsky began to play piano when he was only five years old. His parents decided, however, that a career in the government, rather than the life of a musician, was a far more secure way for their son to make a living. He was therefore trained to become a bureaucrat. Nevertheless, Tchaikovsky continued to play, until his father realized that music rather than government service was his son's true interest. In 1862, Tchaikovsky left his position as a clerk in the government department of justice and attended the new St. Petersburg Conservatory. Over the next three years, he took classes in various aspects of music, including composing. By 1865, his first compositions, a series of dances, were performed outside St. Petersburg. That same year, he graduated from the conservatory and traveled to Moscow to teach music at the Russian Musical Society. Over the next 10 years, he composed symphonies, concertos, operas, and smaller pieces of chamber music. Late in 1875, Tchaikovsky traveled to western Europe and soon afterward completed a ballet, *Swan Lake,* which was performed early in 1877. During the 1880s and 1890s, he continued to compose symphonies and ballets. These included the *Sleeping Beauty* and *Nutcracker* ballets. Tchaikovsky is known for his highly emotional music that creates an immediate response from his audiences. It "conveys the joys, loves, and sorrows of the human heart with striking and poignant sincerity."

to join Grappelli's eightieth birthday concert in Carnegie Hall. The performance was such a success that Ma decided to make a recording with Grappelli in 1989.

The recording was titled *Anything Goes.* This is the name of a piece composed by American songwriter Cole Porter, who was born in Peru, Indiana, in 1893. Cole Porter's family had made a large fortune in the coal and timber businesses. Porter was expected to become a lawyer, and his parents sent him to Yale University in 1909 for an education that would prepare him for the legal profession. Porter had other ideas, though, and enrolled in Yale's School of Music to pursue a career as a songwriter. He began to write songs at Yale, including "Bingo Eli Yale." In 1915, one of his songs, "Hands Up," was included in a Broadway show. Porter then went to Paris, where many American artists and writers lived during the 1920s. He was successful in selling some of his songs and eventually returned to the United States, where he became a popular songwriter. He wrote a variety of hit Broadway musicals, including *Gay Divorce, Anything Goes,* and *Jubilee.* In 1937, he lost the use of his legs after a horseback riding accident. Nevertheless, he continued to compose hit songs until his death in 1964.

Porter wrote many well-known songs during the first half of the twentieth century, including "Just One of Those Things," "I've Got You Under My Skin," and "I Love Paris." He also wrote music for popular shows on Broadway in New York City. The album recorded by Ma and Grappelli featured Porter standards, such as "Anything Goes" and "In the Still of the Night." Yo-Yo Ma enjoyed the experience of playing jazz and continued to explore this type of music.

Next, Ma decided to record an album with the American jazz singer Bobby McFerrin. Born in 1950, McFerrin was trained as a classical pianist. He played in popular bands during the 1970s, however, and finally decided to become a singer. In the early 1980s, McFerrin began to appear as a jazz singer at

Vocalist, composer, and conductor Bobby McFerrin collaborated with Yo-Yo Ma on a 1991 album called *Hush*. Here, McFerrin practices for his performance with young musicians at Fiddlefest, a 2003 concert at Carnegie Hall in memory of violinist Isaac Stern. Yo-Yo Ma also played at the event.

festivals in Hollywood and New York. McFerrin then started a solo jazz act in which he sang and created the sounds of various instruments with his voice.

In 1988, McFerrin attended the Tanglewood Music Festival. Tanglewood is a large estate located in the Berkshire Hills in western Massachusetts, where the Boston Symphony Orchestra began to play during summers in the 1940s. Since that time, the festival has grown into a major musical event, which features classical as well as other forms of music. Each summer, thousands of music lovers travel to Tanglewood to listen to leading performers.

After their first meeting at Tanglewood in 1988, McFerrin and Ma continued to get together at the festival over the next two years. In 1991, they decided to record an album, called *Hush*. It included classical music pieces, several compositions by McFerrin, and his own rendition of "Hush, Little Baby," from which the title of the album was taken. According to author John Attanas, the album "was a smash hit for classical crossover." About the same time, McFerrin recorded another album, called *Play,* which included his hit song "Don't Worry, Be Happy."

8

Working With Young People

Tanglewood is not only the home of great performances. Great musicians like Yo-Yo Ma go to Tanglewood each summer to teach students how to become top-ranked musicians. As Ma once explained, "I can make a contribution . . . I'm renewed." Ma regards his summers at Tanglewood as a place to "relax" from the "hectic profession" of touring and recording classical music.

In a videotape produced at Tanglewood in 1991, Yo-Yo Ma instructed students who came to the Berkshires. These are called "master classes," in which a master performer works with a group of students. In the videotape, Ma encouraged his students to "get to the very deepest core of why you're playing," and admitted, "that's really hard." He also reminded his students that playing takes "incredible concentration." During the videotape, Ma played a piece by Johannes Brahms with the pianist Emmanuel Ax. Ma calls chamber music, "the most intimate form of communication between people." As close friends and performers who have played together many times

Seiji Ozawa conducts a performance at Tanglewood in Lenox, Massachusetts, in 2006.

previously, Ax and Ma communicated very well. Indeed, the performance showed that the two musicians relied only on a smile and a nod of the head to communicate as they performed their music together.

In another part of the videotape, Ma was joined by violinist Isaac Stern and a young Chinese cellist, Jian Wang. Stern has mentored many young performers, including Yo-Yo Ma. He first heard Jian play in Shanghai, when he was only a child. "He touched me," Stern said. "I get excited by talent," Stern added. He not only discovered Jian Wang but also mentored him. "You feel needed," Stern said, by helping young performers "learn how to learn."

WORK WITH CHILDREN

In addition to his classes with students, Yo-Yo Ma also worked with young children. He made guest appearances on programs such as *Sesame Street* and *Mister Rogers' Neighborhood*, explaining music and playing pieces to entertain youngsters. In 1995, he recorded a videotape with trumpeter Wynton Marsalis called *Tackling the Monster*. Marsalis plays both jazz and classical music. The videotape was part of a series made by the trumpeter that was aimed at teaching children how to become musicians.

In *Tackling the Monster*, Marsalis and Ma illustrated 12 principles of how to practice:

1. Seek out private instruction.

2. Write out a schedule to practice all fundamentals of the instrument every day.

3. Set goals to chart your development.

4. Concentrate when practicing.

5. Relax and practice slowly, then play faster and faster.

ASIAN PERFORMERS IN THE UNITED STATES

Jian Wang is one of many Asian performers who have come to the United States to make a successful career in classical music. Wang began to play the cello when he was still a child. He was not only inspired by Isaac Stern but also influenced by Yo-Yo Ma at Tanglewood. During the 1960s and 1970s, students began to arrive from the Far East to play in the United States. They have come from Japan, South Korea, Taiwan, and China. Among them was Yo-Yo Ma, whose parents were Chinese. Stern called Ma "the greatest cellist alive." Another successful classical musician in the 1970s was violinist Cho-Liang Lin from Taiwan. On November 1, 1980, he joined violinist Isaac Stern in a concert at Carnegie Hall.

Many young performers from the Far East have been coming to the United States because there are more symphony orchestras in which to find jobs. In addition, salaries for musicians are higher. They have enrolled in American conservatories, such as the Julliard School in New York City. Japanese conductor Seiji Ozawa, who was formerly the conductor of the Boston Symphony Orchestra, explained that another reason Asian students come to the United States is that they "love to study. It is in our blood."

One of these performers is Wu Man. Born in Hangzhou, China, in 1963, Wu plays the *pipa*—similar to a lute or guitar. She studied the pipa in China but immigrated to the United States in 1990. She plays jazz and crossover music and has performed with many international stars, including Yo-Yo Ma. Wu said that she and other young performers have been greatly influenced by Ma. "Ma is like a big brother to us. He's the greatest communicator I have ever met. He is able to use his music to create connections between people, and teaches us to listen to each other better both as musicians and human beings."

Chinese composer Tan Dun has also been strongly influenced by Yo-Yo Ma. Many of his compositions have been performed by Ma on stage and in film. They work closely together to develop powerful performances that have moved international audiences in many parts of the world. Tan Dun was born in Hunan, China, in 1957. As a teenager, he was named the conductor of his village orchestra. When he was only 22, Tan Dun composed a symphony, called *Li Sao,* which was given a prestigious award by the Chinese government. In 1983, he was also named the winner of a prize for his string quartet. Three years later, Tan Dun came to the United States, where he continued composing music. In 1997, the *New York Times* called him one of the "classical musicians of the year."

Among the best-known performers from the Far East is violinist Midori. Born in 1971, Midori was taught by her mother in Osaka, Japan. She then came to the United States, where she performed at age 11 with the New York Philharmonic. From that performance, she began a highly successful career as a classical music performer. In 2001, she received the Avery Fisher Prize for outstanding achievement in her career. The following year, she celebrated her twentieth season as a performer. Midori has performed across the United States with orchestras in Washington, D.C., Atlanta, San Francisco, Houston, Boston, Chicago, and Seattle. In addition to performances, she has also made numerous recordings of works by Mozart, Tchaikovsky, and many other composers.

Another Asian cellist is Hai-Ye Ni. Like Yo-Yo Ma, she is Chinese. Hai-Ye Ni was born in Shanghai in 1972, where she was taught the cello by her mother. She immigrated to the United States, where she studied in San Francisco. She then won an international cello competition, followed by a performance in York City in 1991. She later toured the United States in 1997 and performed with orchestras across Europe.

Mayuko Kamio is a Japanese violinist. She was born in Osaka, Japan, in 1986 and started to play the violin when she was only four years old. Ms. Kamio appeared on stage for the first time in Tokyo, the capital of Japan, when she was 10. Ms. Kamio then traveled

(continues)

(continued)

to Europe, where she played during her early career. In 2000, she was awarded first place in the Young Concert Artists International Auditions. Eventually, she began to tour the United States, playing in Washington, D.C., in 2001. In 2003, she played at the 92nd Street Y, and two years later appeared at Lincoln Center in New York City. She has also played with the Boston Pops Orchestra.

6. Practice longer on pieces that you cannot play.

7. Play everything with a maximum of expression, always investing yourself, and you will have fun.

8. Do not be too hard on yourself if you make a mistake.

9. Do not show off when you play.

10. Think for yourself.

11. Be optimistic. You do not want pessimism in your music.

12. Look for connections to other things in music.

During the videotape, Yo-Yo Ma admitted that he always hated the thought of practicing. Once he was into it, though, he said, "It's okay." The video production showed Ma working with Marsalis to play the jazz classic "Mood Indigo," which was written by composer and bandleader Duke Ellington.

CLASSICAL PERFORMANCES

During the early 1990s, Yo-Yo Ma made crossover recordings and appeared on videotape, and he also continued to perform classical music. In 1991, for example, he performed the Six Cello Suites at Carnegie Hall, a concert that lasted more than four hours. He performed other concerts in Washington, D.C., and

In 1999, Yo-Yo Ma celebrated the temporary renaming of the corner of East 46th Street and Fifth Avenue in New York to "Yo-Yo Ma Way."

Boston. Before a concert, Ma practiced for many hours, to ensure that he had mastered the music. As he recalled, "you are so into the music that you don't control it any more. You are led by it." Before the concert, he ate very little. "Eating makes you tired, and I was trying to be focused." Finally, all of his preparation was aimed at creating "enough mental as well as physical stamina," to perform at his very best for the audience.

"I am trying to remind myself what I am doing. I am playing the music not to show off or prove anything. I want to share something of what the music means."

Late in 1991, Yo-Yo Ma went on tour in the Far East to To-kyo, Taiwan, and Hong Kong. There he played pieces by Bach and Brahms as well as a composition by modern composer Tod Machover. Machover not only has composed music but also has created what he calls "hyperinstruments," which are "part computer, part conventional instrument." According to writer Thomas Levenson, "They serve as music synthesizers, machines that in theory produce an infinite variety of sounds for compos-ers to use." According to Ma, with a hyperinstrument, "you can make a cello sound like 60 cellos."

As Yo-Yo Ma said in an interview with *Economist* magazine, "Electronic music fascinates me." It gives him another way to relate to an audience. As he expressed it,

> There's something special about developing a rapport with an audience. I never repeat a concert. Every time it's different, and the composition of the audience will be slightly different too. The best kinds of concerts are those in which you are sharing something with an audi-ence. Not "Hey, look at me, I'm a great cellist, see how fast I can play." You're sharing. When those moments happen, you get an out-of-body experience, and you feel that life is worth living.

Yo-Yo Ma added that "I work on developing as many kinds of sounds as possible." This helps him to "renew and reaffirm" what he does.

Perhaps the most unusual audience for which Yo-Yo Ma ever performed assembled for one of his concerts in 1993. That year, he journeyed to the Kalahari Desert in Africa. This vast desert in southern Africa includes large herds of wildlife and an ages-old culture. It had always been a dream of Ma's to play for the people who live there. Finally, he made that dream come true. It was symbolic of Yo-Yo Ma's approach to music—that it should be made available to as broad an audience as possible.

9

New Directions

Yo-Yo Ma is not a musician who confines himself to one type of music—classical, jazz, country, or rock and roll. He plays classical music from the past as well as pieces written by contemporary composers. In addition, his concerts and recordings include music that crosses over the rigid lines that often exist between classical and other types of pieces. Ma believes that all forms of music are related to each other.

MODERN CLASSICS

In 1993, Ma recorded an album called *Made in America*. This recording featured compositions by three twentieth-century American composers: Charles Ives, George Gershwin, and Leonard Bernstein. Ma had played with Bernstein, but both Ives and Gershwin died before Ma was born.

Ma continued with his recording, but he also performed modern and early classical music as part of his busy touring schedule. In 1993, he performed *Memorial of Martin*

Luther King, written by Czech composer Oskar Morawetz. This piece of music was a tribute to the American civil rights leader, who was murdered in 1968. In addition, Yo-Yo Ma performed a piece called *Fire, Water, Paper: A Vietnam Oratorio,* written by twentieth-century American composer Elliot Goldenthal. This composition commemorated the Vietnam War, fought during the 1960s and 1970s, as well as the Vietnam War Memorial built in Washington, D.C., which exhibits the names of all Americans who died in the conflict.

At this time, Ma was also performing standard classical works by earlier composers. In January 1995, he gave a concert featuring works by Johannes Brahms at Carnegie Hall in New York. A day later, Ma traveled to New Haven, Connecticut, where he performed works by Joseph Haydn at Yale University. As part of his busy touring schedule, Ma flew to San Francisco, where he performed a new cello concerto written by twentieth-century composer Richard Danielpour. Later, Ma recorded an album called *Premiers* that included music by Danielpour as well as Leon Kirchner.

In 1995, Ma went to London to appear at London's Barbican Centre, where he played the Six Cello Suites in one evening. His concerts at the Barbican also included works by Beethoven and English composer Sir Edward Elgar. Reviewer Joanne Talbot said that "Ma's fluency with the score produced moments of sheer inspiration." She added that "Ma is [also] an artist dedicated to encouraging young people's interest in music." A few days later he gave a concert for children that included jazz as well as classical selections.

During the 1990s, Yo-Yo Ma continued to be recognized for his outstanding work in the classical music field. He won a series of Grammy Awards; among them was one for a selection of clarinet trios by Brahms, Beethoven, and Mozart that was recorded with Emmanuel Ax and clarinetist Richard Stoltzman. In reference to the clarinet trio by Brahms, one music critic wrote that it was "the best recording of this work to date." In 1998, Ma received a Grammy Award as Artist of the Year.

CONTINUOUS CROSSOVERS

Although Yo-Yo Ma was considered primarily a classical performer, he had not given up his interest in crossover music.

CHARLES IVES (1874–1954), LEONARD BERNSTEIN (1918–1990), AND GEORGE GERSHWIN (1898–1937)

Born in Danbury, Connecticut, in 1874, Charles Ives became one of the leading American composers of the twentieth century. He was the son of George Ives, a band leader in the Union Army during the Civil War. Charles began to play the drum and organ when he was a child, and he practiced as much as four hours a day. He also started to compose music when he was only a teenager. In 1889, he was named organist for a local church and several years later entered Yale University in New Haven, Connecticut, to study music. Although Ives's first love may have been music, he was not sure that he could make a living at it and decided to support himself in the insurance business. Meanwhile, he continued to compose. In June 1908, he married Harmony Twichell, the daughter of a Connecticut minister. He later said, "One thing I am certain of is that, if I have done any good in music, it was, first because of my father, and second, because of my wife." From 1908 until 1920, Ives composed a series of pieces, including two symphonies, violin and piano sonatas, and a string quartet. His works were widely played over the next 30 years, and Ives was awarded a Pulitzer Prize for his music in 1947.

One of the men who popularized Ives's work was Leonard Bernstein. Born in Lawrence, Massachusetts, Bernstein was the son of Jewish immigrants from Russia. After learning to play the piano as a child, Leonard gave music lessons to other children to help earn extra money. He attended Harvard University in the

During his appearances at the Barbican, for example, he had played country music with Mark O'Connor, a well-known country music violin player. O'Connor and Ma were old friends; they met during the concert for Stéphane Grappelli in the late 1980s. Because of his fascination with many types of music, Ma was interested in recording a country album with

1930s and afterward the Curtis Institute of Music in Philadelphia, Pennsylvania. Because of his tremendous talent, he was named as assistant conductor of the New York Philharmonic in 1943. When the conductor suddenly fell ill, Bernstein mounted the podium to lead the orchestra, achieving overwhelming success. Meanwhile he had begun to compose classical music, completing his Symphony no.1: *Jeremiah* in 1943. According to one biographer, he began "virtually reinventing the role of the serious American composer, freely moving between Broadway and the concert hall." He appeared in nightclubs and composed for musicals on stage, while continuing to write classical music. Perhaps his best-known Broadway show was *West Side Story*, which opened in 1957. During the 1950s and 1960s, Bernstein also created a series of television shows, called *Young People's Concerts,* in which he explained classical music to children.

Like Bernstein, George Gershwin also wrote crossover compositions that spanned the classical world as well as other forms of music. Born in New York, he was the son of Jewish immigrants from Russia, as Bernstein was. Gershwin began to play the piano at age 12, concentrating on classical pieces. He also listened to the music of Broadway shows. At age 15, Gershwin was employed to play songs in New York's Tin Pan Alley. Here musicians played new songs on their pianos; the music was heard and purchased by consumers. In 1917, George and his brother Ira wrote "Swanee," which became very popular, selling 2 million records during the 12 months after its release. George Gershwin also wrote music for the movies and Broadway. Among his best-known pieces is *Rhapsody in Blue*, composed in 1924, which combines classical music with jazz.

In 2000, violinist Mark O'Connor (*left*) along with colleagues Edgar Meyer and Yo-Yo Ma (*right*) kick off their Appalachian Journey Tour at the Grand Ole Opry House in Nashville, Tennessee.

O'Connor. During the mid 1990s, the two performers found enough time in their busy schedules to work on a recording.

For Yo-Yo Ma, it was a learning experience. Ma soon realized that, although he was a master of the classical cello, he still had a lot to learn about playing country music. As author John Attanas wrote, "A less secure or more ego-driven musician might have simply packed up his cello and headed home. But this is not Yo-Yo's way. While he has much to teach, he also knows that a good musician never stops learning."

After long rehearsals and many refinements in the music, the musicians finally produced an album in 1996 called *Appalachia Waltz*. It was named after a mountainous region in the eastern United States. Ma praised Sony, the company for which he records albums. "They're committed to the necessity of having a development period for anything they do," he said. Ma explained that he had learned a great deal playing with O'Connor and the third member of their group, Edgar Meyer.

> Edgar has taught me so much about listening, about the sense of time, which is different with this kind of music. It's an exact time—much more exacting than what we do in Haydn, for example. It's a different sense of pulse and I had to learn another kind of bow technique, which is much closer to an older style of playing. . . . From listening to Mark and trying things out, I have far greater accuracy of timing of separate strokes. . . . My foray into this world has led to a complete change in bowing and then to a tighter connection to an earlier period in my own life.

Ma was also praised by his friend Emmanuel Ax for opening up new opportunities for classical music performers. "I think it's great for the rest of us," he said. Ax pointed out that Yo-Yo Ma has made it possible for other classical musicians to do crossover projects. "Fifteen years ago, I probably would have said, 'Yeah, that might be fun, but one shouldn't do that.' Just on that silly basis, I would have said no. I think that people like . . . Yo-Yo are great for the music profession." Ax added, "The whole idea of what music is and what culture and education are has changed so much. Yo-Yo is in a way the right man at the right time. I think we need people like him if music is to remain a truly vital force."

The recording proved to be very popular and sold thousands of albums. New albums do not sell themselves, however. Part of the album's success was due to Ma's status as a superstar, as well as the high quality of the music. Sony also made an enormous effort to market *Appalachia Waltz.* Ma, O'Connor, and Meyer were booked on a seven-concert tour in 1996, including performances on the West and East coasts. The group appeared on a talk show, as well. Sony also marketed the album to a variety of radio stations that specialized in classical and folk music, where the new album was played.

Yo-Yo Ma's crossover music did not end with *Appalachia Waltz.* A follow-up recording, called *Appalachian Journey,* was produced in 2000. This album won a Grammy for Best Classical Crossover Album. Ma also began to explore other types of crossover music. Among these was music for the tango, a popular dance in South America. One of the great tango composers was Astor Piazzolla, a native of Argentina. Born in 1921, Piazzolla and his parents moved to New York City when he was still a child. There he learned to play the bandoneon, similar to an accordion. After his parents moved back to Argentina in the 1930s, Piazzolla continued to play tango music on his bandoneon in Buenos Aires. He also began to write music that mixed tango rhythms with jazz and classical sounds.

In 1997, Yo-Yo Ma recorded *Soul of the Tango* with selections of Piazzolla's music. This recording, like *Appalachia Waltz,* became a hit and won Ma a Grammy for Best Classical Crossover Album. The music was also used for a film, *The Tango Lesson.* To create the album, Ma "spent time in Buenos Aires," wrote Heidi Waleson of *Billboard* magazine, "meeting the musicians who worked with the late tango composer [Piazzolla died in 1989] and going to tango clubs. 'It makes a huge difference in understanding the style,'" according to Ma.

As music critic Barbara Sand added, "In recent years, cellist Yo-Yo Ma has been increasingly pushing a different envelope [taking risks] in a quest to expand the musical universe and in the process make it more accessible to its listeners." Perhaps his most unusual effort to move in a new direction with music was a project called *Inspired by Bach.* Ma had played Bach's cello suites many times, both on stage and on recordings. He was looking for a new way to present the music that might appeal to a wider audience. This led him to a project that involved playing the suites on video as an accompaniment to other activities. The result was six videotapes completed in 1998.

YEOU-CHENG MA

While Yo-Yo Ma's career had reached superstardom, his sister's life had moved in a different direction. Although Yeou-Cheng Ma was a brilliant violinist, she did not enjoy performing the way her brother did. "I was shy and introverted," she admitted. Instead, she decided not to pursue a career as a classical performer. She attended Radcliffe College in Massachusetts, followed by medical school. Yeou-Cheng Ma became a pediatrician who specializes in treating children with hearing and speaking problems. She eventually took a position at a hospital associated with the Albert Einstein College of Medicine in the Bronx, New York. Dr. Ma married Michael Dadap, a conductor, and together they began to run the Children's Orchestra Society in New York. This orchestra had been founded by Dr. Ma's father. By 2005, the Children's Orchestra Society had more than 200 students, 3 orchestras, and 25 chamber groups. Dr. Ma divides her days among the hospital, her two children, and the orchestra. She first tried to teach young musicians when she was 14, assisting her father. "The children were impatient," she said. "I was even more impatient. I figured that teaching wasn't for me." As part of her work with the orchestra, Dr. Ma provides lessons for the children and instructs the chamber music group. Her husband conducts the society's orchestras. According to reporter Anthony Tomasini, Dadap teaches students at all ability levels. "If a beginning student could play only four notes on the . . . violin, Mr. Dadap prepared an arrangement with one part using just those notes." "We really push the limits for ourselves as well as the kids so they extend their potential to its limits," Dr. Ma added. Accompanying the children in these arrangements when they play concerts are such noted musicians as Emmanuel Ax and Yo-Yo Ma.

Yo-Yo Ma originally conceived the idea while attending a conference on Albert Schweitzer, a twentieth-century humanitarian and medical doctor. Schweitzer also played the organ and became an expert on Bach. "His writings on Bach have never gone out of print and I started reading them," Yo-Yo said. "One of the things Schweitzer talked about is that Bach is a pictorial composer—that actually put the bug in my head—who used specific things to tell a story." In one of the videotapes, Ma plays a Bach suite while professional skaters are dancing on ice. Another film features a Bach suite that accompanies efforts to have a new garden built on city-owned land in the center of Boston, Massachusetts. The effort in Boston failed, and the effort to create the garden continued in Toronto, Canada, where it was eventually finished. "It's been a long haul to this special place," said Ma. "But boy, it's worth it."

BACK TO CLASSICAL

Although Yo-Yo Ma was pleased with his crossover projects, he did not neglect his classical music tours. In 1994, he recorded music by Chopin and Beethoven and an album called *Dvorak in Prague: A Celebration.* Ma enjoyed playing works by Dvorak.

Born in Bohemia in 1841, Antonin Dvorak was the son of a local butcher. As a teenager, he received instruction in playing the viola—an instrument similar to the violin, but larger. During the 1850s, Dvorak traveled to Prague, Czechoslovakia, where he continued his musical training and was later hired as a violist by the orchestra of the Prague National Theater. While Dvorak played with the orchestra, he composed music, winning a national award for a symphony in 1874. His work was admired by composer Johannes Brahms, who urged Dvorak to devote himself to writing music. Dvorak composed symphonies, quartets, piano trios, and operas. Many of his pieces were influenced by folk dances native to central Europe.

Yo-Yo Ma also appeared with the Philadelphia Orchestra, playing works by Richard Danielpour, Leon Kirchner, and composer Christopher Rouse. Rouse and Jill Ma had been friends in graduate school, where the composer was introduced to Ma. "He would sit in cafes and write almost without rewriting," Ma recalled.

In 1997, Ma recorded a work by modern American composer Elliot Goldenthal, titled *Fire Water Paper*. The composition, which deals with the horrors of the war in Vietnam, featured Ma on cello, along with a full orchestra and a chorus of adults and children. Late that same year, Ma traveled to Taiwan for a concert that included pieces by Beethoven and eighteenth-century Italian composer Antonio Vivaldi. According to reporter Shirley Fleming,

> When Yo-Yo Ma found out that the festival tickets were expensive and that, in any case, most of them had been sold out weeks in advance, he proposed that rehearsals be open free to students. Eight hundred showed up for the first one and sat quiet as mice for two hours. "He's an idol here," one violinist from Taiwan said.

Yo-Yo Ma continued to maintain a tiring touring schedule. According to one estimate, he plays in 75 concerts per year "and spends one night of every two on the road." He travels without his family, who remain at home. By his own admission, he loves to perform in front of audiences and enjoys the constant challenge of playing different forms of music. As part of his work, Ma made a commercial for Toyota automobiles. He commented:

> This isn't a regular commercial. The car that's being promoted was designed and engineered entirely in Taiwan. For Taiwan, it's a huge thing. They wanted music native to Taiwan, and this tune [that he played in the com-

Yo-Yo Ma smiles after his $2.5-million, 266-year-old cello was returned in 1999 after he mistakenly left it in the trunk of a New York taxi. Police tracked down the cello at a garage in Queens the following day in time for Ma's concert that evening.

mercial] is a song every kid knows. The composer is a professor [here] . . . a wonderful composer. He did a lot of research on Chinese folk music. It's an amazing effort for forty seconds of music.

Yo-Yo Ma might almost be called a workaholic. His schedule seems to be nearly nonstop. It ranges from classical, to jazz, to country, and even to commercials. In fact, Ma's schedule was so strenuous that, one night, after a concert in Carnegie Hall, he lost his cello. Ma plays on a rare cello made during the eighteenth century. It is worth millions of dollars. After leaving Carnegie Hall in October 1999, he hailed a taxi cab, put his cello in the cab's trunk, and jumped into the back seat. After getting out of the cab at his hotel, Ma was so tired that he forgot the cello. Fortunately, Ma knew the number of the cab company, and police helped him track down the driver. By the afternoon of the following day, the police had retrieved the cello. The loss of the cello had hit the local news media, which covered the event. "They have the cello," said one reporter when the police arrived with Ma's instrument. Some people wanted to know why Ma was in a cab rather than an expensive limousine. "I'm like a regular person," he answered. One of his fans, however, said he was much more. "I've heard him play," said Joan Bowden. "It will bring tears to your eyes."

Ma has played three rare cellos. One of them is a Montagnana, made in Italy in the eighteenth century. Another is a Stradivari, made in Italy somewhat earlier. Antonio Stradivari (1644–1737) was one of the world's great makers of violins, cellos, and other instruments. The third instrument that Ma has played is a Goffriller, also an eighteenth-century Italian cello. Ma calls one of his cellos "Petunia." "I was doing a class in Salt Lake City," he recalled, "and a high school student asked if I had a nickname for my cello. I said, 'No, but if I play for you, will you name it?' She chose Petunia, and it stuck."

Yo-Yo Ma (*right*) and Itzhak Perlman perform a piece from the *Memoirs of a Geisha* soundtrack at the 73rd Annual Academy Awards in 2001 in Los Angeles, California.

MUSIC FOR FILMS

Yo-Yo Ma also recorded music for several films during the 1990s. Among them was *Immortal Beloved* in 1994. The film is a biography of world-famous composer Ludwig van Beethoven. Three years later, Ma recorded music for the film *Seven Years in Tibet*—the true story of Austrian mountain climber Heinrich Harrer, who hiked into Tibet in the 1940s. Harrer met the young Dalai Lama, spiritual leader of all Tibetans, and became his tutor. He taught the boy English and broadened his knowledge of world affairs. Finally, in 2000, Ma recorded music for the martial arts film *Crouching Tiger, Hidden Dragon*. The music was written by Chinese composer Tan Dun. An old friend of Ma's, the cellist had recorded another piece by the composer, titled *Heaven, Earth, Mankind*. This music combined Chinese and Western classical music. As one reviewer noted, "Ma is spectacular with the cello." He also recorded the soundtrack for the film *Memoirs of a Geisha*, with Itzhak Perlman, for which he won a Golden Globe Award for Best Original Score in a movie.

10

The Silk Road Project and Other Ventures

The Silk Road refers to a vast network of trade routes begun around 500 B.C. and traveled by merchants for about 1,000 years. Over these routes, precious cargos of silk were carried from China to the West. Silk was highly prized by the wealthy families of Europe; it was used to make fine robes and other garments. There were two main silk routes that ran from central China, one to the north and the other to the south of the vast Gobi Desert in Asia. Then the routes came together and continued through western China across modern Pakistan, through modern Uzbekistan, south of the Caspian Sea to Antioch, which was located in present-day Turkey. From there, silk was transported by ship across the Mediterranean Sea into western Europe. Along the Silk Road, caravans not only brought precious silk. New ideas, such as paper and printing, also were carried from China to the West. Over the Silk Road also came great religious ideas like Christianity, Buddhism, and Islam, as well as music that Yo-Yo Ma turned into popular recordings.

Yo-Yo Ma (*second from left*) and the Silk Road Ensemble perform at Carnegie Hall in New York in 2002. Yo-Yo Ma created the Silk Road Project as a way to study the global circulation of music and musical ideas.

In order to educate listeners about the elements of the Silk Road, the Silk Road Project has published the Silk Road Encounters educational package. According to writer Susan Osmond, it

> . . . includes a sourcebook with background information on the history of the Silk Road and the religions, art, and music spread on its routes; an audio CD sampler in which Silk Road Ensemble musicians discuss their instruments and perform on them; a video in which Ma and ensemble musicians guide students through a musical exploration of the Silk Road; [and] a teachers guide with six model lesson plans. . . . The aim of the multifaceted Silk Road Project is basically

threefold: to illuminate the historical contributions of the Silk Road; support innovative collaborations between composers from Asia, Europe, and North America; and explore classical music within a wider global context.

Being Asian American

For Yo-Yo Ma, the Silk Road symbolized the merging of Eastern and Western cultures, similar to the influences that had shaped his own life. "Throughout my travels," he said, "I have thought about the culture, religions, and ideas that have been influential for centuries along these historic land and sea routes, and I wondered how these complex interconnections occurred and how new musical voices were formed from the diversity of these traditions."

Beginning in 1998, Ma put together the Silk Road Project. For him, perhaps more than any other activity, this project symbolizes what it means to be Asian American. The project brought together musicians and music from countries located along the old Silk Road. These include the modern nations of Uzbekistan, China, Turkey, Lebanon, Iran, Mongolia, and Azerbaijan. As Ma once said, "You don't need a passport or a plane to visit some place new. Music provides a shortcut, allowing you to be transported thousands of miles away and back during the two hour span of a concert. It is this quality of music that is so powerful."

The Silk Road Project presents new pieces especially written for the project at festivals held in a variety of cities, such as Lyon, France; Washington, D.C.; Berkeley, California; and cities across Asia. All of the festivals in the United States have been sold out. The musical pieces are written by composers from countries along the Silk Road as well as new works by well-known modern composers, such as Richard Danielpour and Tan Dun.

MA'S OTHER ACTIVITIES

Although devoting himself to the Silk Road Project, Yo-Yo Ma still found time for many other activities. In 2000, he attended the World Cello Congress, held at Towson University, in Maryland. As part of the Congress, Ma gave a master class

At these festivals, Yo-Yo Ma has been joined by musicians who play instruments from nations along the trade route. These instruments include a Mongolian *morin khur,* a fiddle with two strings, played by Ma. "I can assure you, having fewer strings doesn't make it twice as easy," he said. Another native instrument is the pipa, a lute (early guitar) from China. One of the pieces played by the Silk Road Ensemble was Concerto for Pipa and Strings, by an American composer, Lou Harrison. Another piece, *The Silent City,* was written by Iranian composer Kayhan Kalhor. Explaining the meaning of his work, Kalhor said it commemorates "all cities that are somehow destroyed because of human mistakes or selfishness."

In 2002, Ma and the other musicians recorded *Silk Road Journeys: When Strangers Meet.* "Every time I open a newspaper, I am reminded that we live in a world where we can no longer afford not to know our neighbors," said Ma. "The Silk Road Project is a musical way to get to know your neighbors." In 2006, the Silk Road musicians played at the Virginia Arts Festival. Speaking of Ma's commitment to the project, Rob Cross, director of the festival, said, "It shows he's not willing to sit back on his success. For him, this project is a labor of love. He does this because he cares so much about music." Ma added: "I just feel more human. I feel that I belong in the world. We've all grown a lot and we each feel like we're a part of the world."

Yo-Yo Ma performs during the Dan David Prize award ceremony at Tel Aviv University, in Israel in 2006. Ma received a prestigious and valuable prize, worth $1 million, in recognition for his Silk Road Project's contribution to international cultural understanding. In his acceptance speech, Ma said he would share the money with the musicians, board members, and staff of the project.

for eight young students. He worked with one student, Mike Block, urging him to "stretch" his musical performance to the ultimate. "Good, good," Ma said after Block had performed. "Was there anything different?" he asked the audience, which was applauding. "How did you feel?" he asked Block. "I felt stronger," Block answered.

Yo-Yo Ma also went on tour with Mark O'Connor and Edgar Meyer to promote their album *Appalachian Journey,* released as a follow-up to *Appalachia Waltz.* In addition, Ma's new album, called *Solo,* was released by Sony Records. It included a variety of pieces written for solo cello. Some were traditionally classical music, whereas other compositions were crossovers. As Ma put it, "Music that we categorize as 'classical' is actually kind of a global music without putting it into another category of world music." Among the pieces included on the new disk are works from China, "Appalachia Waltz" by O'Connor, and music by twentieth-century Hungarian composer Zoltán Kodály. Music critic David Moore reviewed the album; he wrote that Ma's recording was "the most moving performance and programming of the Kodály I have ever heard."

As a result of his appearances and his recordings, Yo-Yo Ma was one of the most famous musicians in America and around the world. During an interview with *Time* Magazine, Ma was asked if he enjoyed all the recognition that he receives as a superstar performer. He said that his favorite incidents

> . . . are moments of non-recognition. A few years ago, I was on a plane with a cello. She [his cello] gets the window seat, and I'm scrunched up in the middle next to a large man asking the usual questions—'Do you play professionally?'—and finally he says, 'What's your name?' I say, 'Yo-Yo Ma.' 'Not possible. I know what that is, and Yo-Yo Ma is a woman.' I took out my driver's license to show him. I still don't think he believed me.

TRAGEDIES OF 2001

In 2001, Yo-Yo Ma's career was impacted by two tragedies. The massive terrorist attacks of September 11 on the World Trade Towers in New York and the Pentagon in Washington, D.C., filled not only Ma but also much of the world with horror. Fewer than two weeks later, violinist Isaac Stern died. Stern had been one of Ma's mentors and a close friend. On September 30, Yo-Yo Ma appeared at a memorial concert for Stern and later that day participated in a Concert of Remembrance, recalling the lives of the people killed during the terrible attacks of September 11. At this concert he played "Appalachia Waltz" and a Bach cello suite.

NEW VENTURES

Over the next two years, Ma's busy schedule continued, with time in between to spend with his family. Both of his children seemed to have inherited a gift for music. His daughter, Emily, plays violin and piano, and his son, Nicholas, plays piano. "When they're home," Ma said of his two teenage children, "you hear them singing all the time. It's great. It's a nice part of their lives, and you know that something's percolating inside." Ma added that his children also have a greater appreciation now for the music that he plays. In the past, Emily fell asleep at his concerts. As Ma said, "She used to say, 'Daddy, it's not that I don't like to hear you play, but it's dark in the hall and I get so sleepy and so comfy.' But she's beyond that now. I think she does stay awake."

In 2002, Yo-Yo Ma was honored with the National Medal of Arts Award in Washington, D.C. At the ceremony he accompanied Condoleezza Rice, then the national security advisor to President George Bush, who played the piano. The following year, at an event in Carnegie Hall, Ma had a chance to play a unique concert with a young girl halfway around the world. She was recorded while singing a song in China, and her image was beamed to New York, where it was played on a video screen. Then Ma accompanied the girl's voice with his cello. As reporter Susan Jakes wrote, "He listens, eyes shut and eyebrows raised, to each line of her high-pitched call, then plunges his bow to answer in peals of sonorous, throaty yearning." The song was recorded by the Chinese composer Tan Dun, and he told the girl that it would be sent far away. "All the way to Beijing [capital of China]?" she asked. "To the other side of the earth," replied Tan, "where there is a beautiful musician who plays as beautifully as

Yo-Yo Ma performed in 2001 at the Concert of Remembrance at
New York's Carnegie Hall, in honor of those affected by the September 11
terrorist attacks.

you sing. Imagine you're playing to him, and that he plays back to you." When Yo-Yo Ma saw the tape the first time, he said, "I hope I can meet this girl and play with her."

MA'S HITS AND THE STATE OF CLASSICAL MUSIC

In 2006, the *New York Times* listed some of Yo-Yo Ma's best albums:

- *Simply Baroque II*; recorded in 2000 on instruments like those used in the Baroque period (seventeenth century)
- *Obrigado Brazil*
- *Bach: Six Unaccompanied Cello Suites*
- *Made in America*; music by Ives, Gershwin, Kirchner, and Bernstein
- *Great Cello Concertos*; includes music by Dvorak, Saint-Saëns, Haydn, and Elgar
- *Soul of the Tango*; music by Astor Piazzolla
- *Silk Road Journeys: When Strangers Meet*

Regardless of Yo-Yo Ma's success, classical CDs often do not sell as well as rock-and-roll music CDs. There are also far more radio stations that play rock and roll than classical music. Nevertheless, classical music still remains quite popular. Each year, an estimated 1,800 classical music orchestras play for audiences across the United States. They presented about 36,000 concerts annually—almost a third more than a decade ago. Many people also download classical pieces from the Internet to play on their iPods. Classical music concerts are regularly sold out, like those at Carnegie Hall, the 92nd Street Y, and Lincoln Center in New York City. Special music festivals are also very popular, such as Mostly Mozart, Tanglewood, and the Aspen Music Festival in Colorado. As Allan Kozinn of the *New York Times,* expressed it, "Rumors of classical music's demise haven't just been exaggerated, they've been dead wrong." Asked about the state of classical music, Yo-Yo Ma said he was optimistic about the future.

During 2003, Ma played a new concerto composed by Tan Dun, called *The Map*. This was the music of China. Ma and the Boston Symphony Orchestra accompanied a videotape produced by Tan Dun that included Chinese musicians playing centuries-old instruments. Ma provided the cello music, a "solo cello line . . . [that] has a lilting and sometimes soaring quality that draws on the characteristic sweetness of Mr. Ma's sound . . ." according to *New York Times* music critic Allan Kozinn.

Later in the year, Yo-Yo Ma performed an entirely different type of music in New York City. These were compositions from a newly released album, *Obrigado Brazil*. They included pieces from Latin America, among them compositions by Astor Piazzolla and the Brazilian pianist and composer Antonio Carlos Jobim. The *Obrigado Brazil* album won 3 Grammy Awards, bringing Ma's total Grammy wins to 15.

CONSTANT IMPROVEMENT

Yo-Yo Ma never seems content with his performances, and he is always trying to improve. To help improve his playing, Ma began to use a tape recorder when he was still a child. His father introduced the tape recorder into the Ma household in New York during the 1960s. Young Yo-Yo became accustomed to listening to his performances as they were recorded on tape, so he and his father could critique them. Ma has used the tape recorder for many years to evaluate his own playing. He began by putting a tape recorder in the back of a large music hall to find out how people in the back heard the sounds of his cello. He said:

> Now the thing that is really hard to do, that I think may be one of the hardest things to do, is to be in one place and somewhere else at the same time, which means to be empathetic to another space other than your own. What I learned from hearing recordings from, let's say,

President George W. Bush (*left*) shakes hands with Yo-Yo Ma (*right*) after his performance with U.S. National Security Adviser Condoleezza Rice, (*center*) at the National Endowment for the Arts National Medal of Arts Awards ceremony in 2002 in Washington.

a mike that was placed at 20 feet versus 60 feet away is it makes the tempo sound different. It makes what you think may have been the right speed to do something— it may be wrong by the time you go 60 feet away. You can only really know that when there's evidence. And a tape recorder actually gives you that evidence.

This is another example of Ma's concern for his listeners. As his friend Emmanuel Ax put it, ". . . one of the things that really distinguishes him from a lot of performers is that he really feels a connection with the audience and audiences are very important to him."

Ma seemed just as much at home in front of an audience whether he was playing the songs of Latin America or the classical music of German composer Richard Strauss. Yo-Yo Ma performed with the Philadelphia Orchestra in October 2004. As Anthony Tommasini, music critic for the *New York Times* wrote, "Mr. Ma played with his customary command and vibrancy." Early in 2005, Yo-Yo appeared at Lincoln Center, playing a piece by Chinese composer Chen Yi. It was entitled *Ballad, Dance and Fantasy*. According to *New York Times* music critic Bernard Holland, "Chen Yi's music is about storytelling and theater. . . . Mr. Ma's long, overarching solos are the storytellers here . . . [his playing is] in imitation of traditional Chinese stringed instruments." Holland concluded that Yo-Yo Ma was "very good."

The concert at Lincoln Center reflected Ma's commitment to the international aspects of music. In 2005, the Silk Road Ensemble issued a new album, *Silk Road Journeys: Beyond the Horizon*. It featured playing by the cello, the pipa, and other instruments from across the globe. Among the pieces of music was "Akhalqalaqi Dance," a folk song from Armenia in central Europe. In addition, there were two pieces from Azerbaijan. Early in 2006, Yo-Yo Ma received important recognition for his work in the international world of music. He was awarded the annual Dan David Prize for one million dollars for contributing to "cultural heritage protection" with the Silk Road Project. Asked if the Silk Road Project had changed his way of playing, Ma said, "Absolutely. Playing with Persians and Turks, I realized that for the past 40 years I've been rushing. Forget notes and how you articulate them—think about space. Now I play Haydn differently, and I play Bach differently."

As Ma's close friend Emmanuel Ax once said, "You see people who are fantastic communicators, but they may not be at the very top of musical ability. And you see great players who are maybe kind of withdrawn and they commune with the music and the audience is welcome to watch. . . . And then you have Yo-Yo."

CHRONOLOGY

1955 Yo-Yo Ma is born in Paris, France.
1962 Comes to the United States; plays at the
National Armory in Washington, D.C. with
his sister; Becomes a student of
Leonard Rose.
1970 Graduates from high school; attends
Meadowmount.

TIMELINE

1978
Ma wins the
Avery Fisher
Prize.

1962
Ma comes to the
United States.

1955

1985

1955
Yo-Yo Ma is born
in Paris, France.

1985
Ma wins his first
Grammy Award for the
Bach cello sonatas.

1971
Ma makes his debut
at Carnegie Hall.

1971 Performs in concert at the United Nations; makes his debut at Carnegie Hall.

1972 Enters Harvard University.

1976 Graduates from Harvard University.

1977 Marries Jill Hornor.

1978 Wins the Avery Fisher Prize; appears at the Mostly Mozart Festival.

1980 Undergoes successful surgery for scoliosis; begins regular performances with Emmanuel Ax.

1985 Wins his first Grammy Award; records with Claude Bolling.

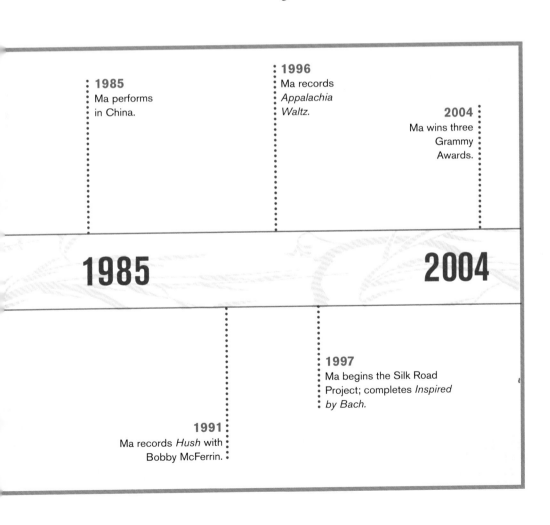

1985
Ma performs in China.

1996
Ma records *Appalachia Waltz.*

2004
Ma wins three Grammy Awards.

1985 **2004**

1997
Ma begins the Silk Road Project; completes *Inspired by Bach.*

1991
Ma records *Hush* with Bobby McFerrin.

1986–1987 Wins additional Grammy Awards; performs in China.

1991 Makes a recording with jazz violinist Stéphane Grappelli; records *Hush* with Bobby McFerrin.

1993 Performs in the Kalahari Desert in Africa.

1996 Records *Appalachia Waltz*.

1997 Records *Soul of the Tango*.

1998 Completes *Inspired by Bach;* begins the Silk Road Project.

2000 Records music for *Crouching Tiger, Hidden Dragon*.

2002 Records *Silk Road Journeys: When Strangers Meet*.

2003 Records a concerto by Chinese composer Tan Dun; releases *Obrigado Brazil*.

2004 Wins three Grammy Awards.

2005 Releases *Silk Road Journeys: Beyond the Horizon*.

GLOSSARY

bandoneon—An instrument similar to an accordion.

cantata—A piece of music for instruments and singers.

chamber music—Classical music performed by small groups of musicians.

Chinese Exclusion Act—An act passed by the U.S. government in 1882, limiting Chinese immigration.

chorale—A piece of music for a choir.

composition—The creation of a new, original piece of music.

concerto—A piece of music written for an orchestra and usually featuring one instrument, like violin, piano, or cello.

encroach—To intrude.

measure—A segment of musical time made up of beats, set off by bar lines.

morin khur—A Mongolian fiddle.

oratorio—A large piece of choral music.

overture —Musical introduction to a play or opera.

pavane—A popular dance in European courts.

philharmonic—A large symphony orchestra.

pipa—A lute from China.

prelude—A short piece of music that serves as an introductory piece.

prodigy—An extraordinarily talented individual.

quartet—A piece of music written for four instruments or a group of four instruments.

quintet—A piece of music written for five instruments or a group of five instruments.

respite—A rest or pause.

scoliosis—Curvature of the spine.

suite—A piece of music for a single instrument.

solo—A musical composition for one voice or instrument.

sonata—An instrumental piece in several movements for soloists or small ensembles.

symphony—A large orchestra, or a piece of music of about four parts written for a large orchestra.

trio—A piece of music written for three instruments or a group of three instruments.

viola—An instrument similar to the violin but larger.

violincello—The original name for the instrument commonly called the cello.

virtuoso—An outstanding musician.

BIBLIOGRAPHY

Attanas, John. *Yo-Yo Ma: A Life in Music.* New York: John Gordon Burke Publisher, 2003.

Blum, David. *Quintet.* Ithaca, N.Y.: Cornell University Press, 1998.

Ma, Marina. *My Son, Yo-Yo.* Hong Kong: The Chinese University Press, 1995.

Ma, Yo-Yo. *Yo-Yo Ma at Tanglewood.* Video. New York: A Third Eye Production, 1991.

Marsalis, Wynton, and Yo-Yo Ma. *Tackling the Monster.* Video. New York: Sony Music Entertainment, 1995.

FURTHER READING

BOOKS

Ashley, Susan. *Yo-Yo Ma.* New York: World Almanac Library, 2005.

Chippendale, Lisa. *Yo-Yo Ma: A Cello Superstar Brings Music to the World.* Berkeley Heights, N.J.: Enslow, 2004.

Gan, Geraldine. *Lives of Notable Asian Americans: Arts, Entertainment, Sports.* Philadelphia: Chelsea House, 1995.

Olmstead, Mary. *Yo-Yo Ma.* New York: Raintree, 2006.

ARTICLES

Jakes, Susan. "Yo-Yo Ma Taking a Flight on a Musical Journey Without Borders." *Time* (2003).

Levenson, Thomas. "Taming the Hypercello." *The Sciences* (1994).

Rubinstein, Leslie. "Oriental Musicians Come of Age." *New York Times* (1980).

Zuckerman, Eugenia. "Stradivari's Genius: The Master Builder." *New York Times* (2005).

WEB SITES

"Biography: Leonard Bernstein." Bernstein's Studio. Available online. URL:http://www.leonardbernstein.com/lifeswork/biography.

Ormond, Susan. "Yo-Yo Ma's Silk Road Project." Worldandi.com. Available online. URL:http://www.worldandi.com/public/2002/april/silkintro.html.

The Silk Road Project. Available online. URL:http://www.silkroadproject.org/events/festivals.html.

PHOTO CREDITS

INDEX

ABOUT THE AUTHOR

RICHARD WORTH is a writer and corporate trainer with more than 25 years of experience writing young-adult nonfiction. He has published more than 50 books in biography, history, current events, and the criminal justice system. His book *Gangs and Crime* was included on the New York Public Library's Best Books for the Teen Age list. Some of his other books include *American Slave Trade, Plantation Life, Africans in America,* and *Colonial America.*